BASKETRY

BASKETRY

A WORLD GUIDE TO TRADITIONAL TECHNIQUES

ONE

TWO

THREE

FOUR

FIVE

BRYAN SENTANCE

WITH 833 ILLUSTRATIONS, 697 IN COLOUR

Thames & Hudson

The baskets illustrated in this book range in height from very small (1 cm, ³⁄₈ in.) to very large (200 cm, 78 in.), but the majority are between 10 cm (4 in.) and 50 cm (20 in.) high.

PAGE 1: *Hat, from Zimbabwe, decorated with strips of plastic sacking salvaged from irrigation projects.*
PAGE 2: *Baskets, from around the world, made of natural fibres.*
PAGE 3: *Plaited bag from the Solomon Islands.*
PAGE 5: *Coiled grass statuette of the Hindu god Ganesh, overcomer of obstacles, from Bihar, India.*
PAGE 6: ABOVE, RIGHT: *Plaited birch bark basket from Finland.*
BELOW, LEFT: *Coiled pandanus basket from Darién, Panama.*
PAGE 7: TOP: *Cassava strainers from Central Africa.*
MIDDLE: *Cherokee twilled basket from southeastern USA.*
BOTTOM: *Twined grass hat from Ghana.*

Designed by David Fordham

First published in the United Kingdom in 2001 by Thames & Hudson Ltd,
181A High Holborn, London WC1V 7QX

www.thamesandhudson.com

First paperback edition 2007

British Library Cataloguing-in-Publication Data
A catalogue record for this book is available from the British Library
ISBN-13: 978-0-500-28670-8
ISBN-10: 0-500-28670-1

Printed and bound in Singapore by C.S. Graphics

"Blessed shal be thy bazkett and thy stoare"

Deuteronomy xxviii, 5
Coverdale Bible, 1535

CONTENTS

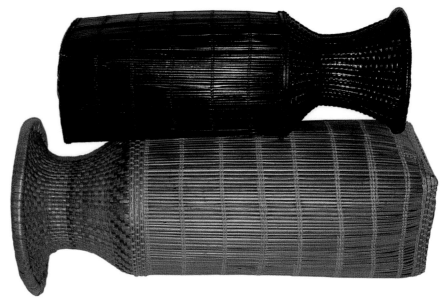

INTRODUCTION

BASKETRY is in one sense the most humble of crafts, employed through the millennia to produce functional objects that feature in all aspects of the everyday life of ordinary people. Yet the care and ingenuity taken in the making of traditional baskets has endowed them with an intrinsic beauty which provides the modern artist and designer with a treasure house of inspiration. The variety is astonishing and basketry ranges from the pure, practical forms of plaited Cambodian rice steamers, through the symbolic motifs on mats from Sarawak, to the flamboyance of Californian featherwork gift baskets. Although the modern world offers much in the way of alternative choices, few homes are without some form of basket. They still provide us with a link to the natural world and a more natural lifestyle.

THE STORY OF THE SUN BASKET

*I*N *the beginning there was no land and Oncoyeto floated above the water in the form of a white feather. At last, becoming restless, he landed on the water and it whirled round like a whirlpool making a great heap of froth. From the foam Oncoyeto made an island and parted the water from the land.*

Now Oncoyeto took the shape of a man, but still he was not satisfied, for all was darkness. When he looked up, he could see stars twinkling far away in the sky and so he decided to set out on a long journey to learn how to make light.

At last Oncoyeto arrived at the star country. Here the people made him welcome, but he could not see where the light came from. He searched high and low; he looked everywhere. But there

ABOVE: *Yuki 'sun basket' decorated with feathers and abalone shells, from California, or Utah, USA.*
LEFT: *Southern Paiute (Kaibab) Native Americans equipped with baskets for gathering foodstuffs.*
OPPOSITE: *Grass basket from Colombia, commissioned by TUMI, a fair trade organization.*

ABOVE, LEFT: *Ivy,* Hedera helix. *The tree once strangled by the ivy has decayed, leaving a natural basket.*
ABOVE, RIGHT: *Stems of a mature wisteria twined around a gazebo in the Royal Botanic Gardens at Kew, Surrey, England.*

was one place he was not allowed to go. He could not enter the sweat lodge which only the sick were permitted to enter. This surely must be the place where the light was kept.

One day the people of the bright land announced that they were going hunting. Oncoyeto feigned sickness. The old men took Oncoyeto to the sacred sweat lodge that he might be cured by its powerful medicine. As he stepped inside, he was blinded by the light, for hanging from the roof poles were baskets and in each one was a bright shining sun.

Oncoyeto could hardly contain his excitement. He waited until the old men became drowsy and one by one fell asleep. At last he leapt up and grabbed the basket containing the brightest sun. Swiftly, he fled and relentlessly he was pursued by the people of the bright land, but Oncoyeto was the fastest and at last he reached home safely.

Oncoyeto hung the sun basket in the sky far in the east. Yet it did not cast its light as he wished and he moved it higher in the sky. Still it did not please him. Again he moved it – and again and again.

Oncoyeto never could find the right place and he is moving the sun basket to this day.

The legend of Oncoyeto is told by the Yuki people of California who still make beautiful 'sun baskets' covered with feathers. But the story tells us something else – the first baskets were not made in living memory, or even in historic times, but so long ago that they come from the realms of myth, from the very dawn of time. We do not know precisely when the first baskets were made, but some of the earliest ceramics found in Mesopotamia, dating to about 3,000 BC, bear the imprints of mats and baskets upon their surface.

THE ORIGINS OF BASKETS

I T could be said that Mother Nature was the first basketmaker – look at the way honeysuckle winds itself around a trellis, how wisteria twines and how ivy weaves over and under, round its own tendrils, until it throttles its host. Look at spiders' webs – each species of spider has its own style of web, beautifully made anew each morning. Look at birds' nests – they may at first appear haphazard, but watch a weaverbird in action. Using only its beak, the male bird skilfully weaves each strand of grass carefully in and out, one at a time, to build up a thin-walled, hollow nest with a tubular entrance dangling from the frond of a palm. He may even have to build several, since the females choose only the best weavers to father their chicks.

Our distant relatives, the apes, also weave. Every night a chimpanzee will climb a suitable tree to make a nest out of the reach of predators. They bend over branches and weave them together to create a secure platform before covering it with leaves, making a comfortable bed.

The interlaced grass nest of the Baya weaverbird, from Thailand.

ABOVE, LEFT: *A basket of folded birch bark for gathering sap or berries from Archangel on Russia's White Sea coast.*
ABOVE, RIGHT: *This Samoan 'ato, plaited from a single intact coconut frond, is used to carry freshly gathered fruit and vegetables. The basket is plaited around its contents, and is cut open and thrown away once it is no longer needed.*
BELOW: *An ingenious hat being plaited from a palm frond on Fiji.*

THE EARLIEST BASKETS

To imagine what kind of baskets our ancestors first made, we must look to surviving hunter-gatherer societies, whose lifestyle has changed very little for millennia, and also at baskets spontaneously assembled for immediate use. Hunter-gatherers travel light, uncluttered by possessions, and are expert at making what they need from the materials immediately to hand. In the forests of Finland and northern Russia, makeshift receptacles for collecting the sap of birch trees are constructed by folding a piece of birch bark and pinning it in place with a twig. The Aborigines of Australia's Northern Territory make simple baskets using a very similar technique.

The leaflets of a palm frond, since they are attached at one end, are ideal for an impromptu, disposable, plaited basket or hat. In Samoa baskets such as the *'ato* are regularly constructed from a coconut frond plaited around its intended burden. Upon arrival at home or at the market, the *'ato* is cut open along the rib to release the contents and the basket is thrown away. It has even been suggested by Jack Lenor Larson that the invention of basketry made it possible for our ancestors to eat communally rather than at the food source, possibly leading to the development of communication skills and language.

The craft of weaving baskets intended for long-term use was most probably developed around 12,000 years ago, at the same time as the first agricultural methods and the establishment of settled communities, because it is in these places that the oldest surviving woven artefacts have been found.

SUMERIAN PRIEST-KING CARRYING A BASKET

HISTORICAL EVIDENCE

Very little ancient basketry remains. Humble, workaday objects such as baskets have always been thrown away when they are no longer serviceable. As basketry involves the use of perishable materials, they will normally disintegrate and only survive the passage of centuries under exceptional circumstances. The oldest known remains are fragments of coiled basketry used for the lining of grain stores at Fayum in Egypt. These were preserved because of the dry desert sand and subsequently dated by Sir William Flinders Petrie to the pre-Dynastic period (10,000–8,000 BC). Ancient twined fragments were also discovered in Fishbone Cave, Utah, in the arid American West, dating back to as early as 9250 BC, around the end of the last Ice Age.

At archaeological sites around the world there is evidence of the use of basketry since their first occupation. Coiled grain baskets were discovered in Turkey at Çatal Hüyük, the second oldest city in the world, which was founded in 6250 BC.

Among the earliest known communal habitations in England was the Lake Village at Glastonbury in Somerset. Here, preserved in the mud since the Early Iron Age, the remains of wattle panels used for the walls of the houses were found.

In the American Southwest, in Arizona, Utah and Nevada, the oldest sites were once occupied by a mysterious people known to the Navajo as the Anasazi ('the old ones'). Because of the quality and quantity of baskets and fibre sandals discovered here, archaeologists dubbed the periods of occupation as Basketmaker I (AD 100–400) and Basketmaker II (AD 400–700). The pottery at this time was only rudimentary.

Sometimes information about basketmaking and its uses can be gathered from secondary sources, such as stone carving, mural paintings or ancient texts. A votive limestone plaque from around 3,000 BC can be seen in the Louvre, Paris; it depicts Ur-Nină, the first Sumerian priest-king of Babylon, carrying a basket on his head. On the walls of the mortuary temple of Hatshepsut (built between 1473 and 1458 BC), at Deir el-Bahri across

TOP: EGYPTIANS CARRYING A TREE IN A ROD-COILED BASKET, AFTER A PAINTING AT DEIR EL-BAHRI, THEBES

ABOVE: ASSYRIANS FERRYING A CHARIOT ACROSS THE RIVER TIGRIS, AFTER A STONE RELIEF DATING FROM 860 BC

ABOVE, LEFT: *Anasazi sandals, from* Aboriginal Indian Basketry *by Otis Tufton Mason (1902).*
LEFT: *Makah basketmakers of Washington State, USA, in the 1890s.*
RIGHT: *Nellie Salmon, a Umatillo girl with a Nez Perce corn-husk bag decorated with false embroidery, USA, c. 1900.*
OPPOSITE: *George Wharton James, the author of* Indian Basketry *(1901), describing the Navaho sacred basket.*

LEFT: AN AZTEC BRIDAL
COUPLE SITTING TOGETHER
ON A MAT, AFTER THE
SIXTEENTH-CENTURY
CODEX MENDOZA

BELOW, LEFT: ST GUTHLAC
BUILDING HIS CHURCH, AFTER
A MEDIEVAL MANUSCRIPT.
HE IS DEPICTED HOISTING
MATERIALS IN A BASKET.

COILED STRAW
BEE SKEPS, AFTER
A MEDIEVAL
MANUSCRIPT

the River Nile from Luxor in Egypt, are paintings of the great trading mission to the Land of Punt. Two men are shown carrying a precious incense-bearing tree slung between them in a rod-coiled basket. For literary evidence of basketmaking we can consult many sources, including Herodotus (b. 484 BC), known as the 'father of history', who described many items, such as the round basketwork boats that were used on the River Tigris.

In spite of the lack of physical evidence, many sources of information about daily life in the past survive and we are able to glean a good sense of the important roles of basketry. For example, we are able to witness the agricultural methods of European farm labourers and builders in medieval illuminated manuscripts, as well as the religious practices of the Aztecs in codices compiled by the Conquistadores.

THE STUDY OF BASKETS

UNTIL the beginning of the twentieth century, little interest was taken by academics in the study of baskets. In fact, they were virtually ignored. Captain James Cook made three voyages around the Pacific between 1768 and 1780 and collected much information and many artefacts, but comments in the journals of Cook and his crew state only that coconut and pandanus baskets were made 'in a thousand different designs' and for 'multifarious purposes'. They did not collect any.

It has been suggested that perhaps baskets were too humble, or too familiar to be taken seriously, or even that they were ignored because basketmaking was women's work. Archaeology had been for most a glorified treasure hunt, a search for works of art to line the houses of the rich, an approach that lasted until the advent of a new breed of archaeologist, men such as Flinders Petrie, who were interested in the everyday life of people.

The publication of *Aboriginal Indian Basketry* by Otis Tufton Mason in 1902 – a paper written to describe the collection in the Smithsonian Institution, Washington, D.C. – and of *Indian Basketry* by George Wharton James in 1909, meant that for the first time the humble craft was accepted as a subject worth investigating and recording. Since then the race has been on to collect as much information and as many baskets as possible before it is too late.

TWILIGHT BASKETRY?

I T is now cheaper and easier to buy a plastic bucket than to make a basket. Learning to make baskets takes time and patience. The financial returns are too small if you have a family to feed or the bright lights are calling. But basketmaking is one way in which cultures, beliefs and traditional values can be kept alive. There are still those, perhaps even a growing number, who have realized the spiritual benefits of working with their hands, though in many places traditional basketry is a dying craft.

In too many cultures the young have not learned the traditional skills. In a trading post in Prescott, Arizona, I photographed a fine Yavapai basket. Todd Calhoon, the proprietor, told me sadly that it had been made in 1980 by Effie Starr, who had died eight years later aged 78. There were at most two or three good Yavapai basketmakers left, all in their twilight years.

In some countries crafts projects have been set up to keep the old skills alive. H.M. the Queen of Thailand, for one, has provided inspiration and training in the technique of weaving with the *Yan lipao* vine. Elsewhere charitable organizations, such as Oxfam and Tumi, have provided money and employment by commissioning baskets for export. Meanwhile, in the Philippines, basketmaking is a thriving industry – cheap products are churned out for the Western market.

ABOVE: *The ceiling of the Hubbell trading post at Ganado, Arizona. Traders like the Hubbells accumulated impressive collections of Native American basketry.*
NEAR RIGHT: *A fine Yavapai coiled basket made by Effie Starr at the age of seventy.*

BASKETRY AND ECOLOGY

T RADITIONAL basketmakers are true conservationists. If they are to be sure of a supply of materials to ply their craft, they must take only what they need and only what the plant can spare. Basketmakers in the Aleutian Islands specialize in fine-twined grass baskets. They harvest the grass, *Elymus mollis*, selectively, a single blade at a time. When the Maoris collect *harakeke* (phormium) leaves they never cut the ones in the centre as this is the growing part of the plant which will supply their future needs. All the trimmings are scattered to act as a mulch.

ABOVE: *Twined grass basket, from the Aleutian Islands, decorated with false embroidery.*

In many cultures the plant is not only treated with great respect, but it is also seen as a spiritual entity that needs to be nurtured and placated. Thus the gathering of materials and the making of a basket are accompanied by prayer, ritual and taboo. There were once so many taboos on basketweaving among the Navajo, including a ban on sexual intercourse, that for a long time many women abandoned the craft altogether, preferring to trade for them with their neighbours, the Paiutes.

Because they work so closely with nature, basketmakers are among the first to notice changes in the environment. Whether because of pollution, climate change or the change in land use, they constantly need to adapt their working methods if they are to keep their craft alive. Some Aleutian basketmakers, for example, are now forced to travel several hours by plane to find a source of suitable materials, while in England, at East Mersea in Essex, the oyster tendle can no longer be made from the traditional green elm saplings, since the trees were annihilated by Dutch elm disease in the 1960s.

ABOVE: *An Aleutian basketmaker working on a twined grass basket in the 1890s.*
BELOW: *Plaited basket used to store tobacco by old Kuba men in the Democratic Republic of Congo.*

ABOVE: *Oyster tendle; they were made from elm until the devastation caused by Dutch elm disease in the 1960s and 1970s.*

We live, at the beginning of a new millennium, in a throw-away society. When we no longer need something, we discard it. We wrap and package food and consumables, and then throw away the packing. Our packaging comes from non-sustainable sources; its production pollutes our atmosphere and non-biodegradable junk piles high on our rubbish tips.

In a sense, we have always been a throw-away society. The difference is what we throw away today. As little as fifty years ago, if it was not in a can, virtually everything was packaged in paper or basketry. Many things, from yeast to field-gun cartridges, were packed in a basket. The baskets were made from extensive renewable sources, the atmosphere was not polluted by their production and, when the basket was thrown away, it rotted down and helped enrich the soil.

It is time we confronted our indulgent devastation of our world. Perhaps if more of us were to learn an honest craft like basketmaking, our eyes would be opened and we would become more sensitive to the precarious balance of our environment.

ABOUT THIS BOOK

IT was not my aim to write a manual. It is my intention, by giving a simple analysis of structure and use and by juxtaposing images of basketry from distant places, to provide a basis for comparison and therefore appreciation of the skill of some of the world's most inventive, but undervalued, craftspeople. It is my great regret that space has allowed only this small representative sample.

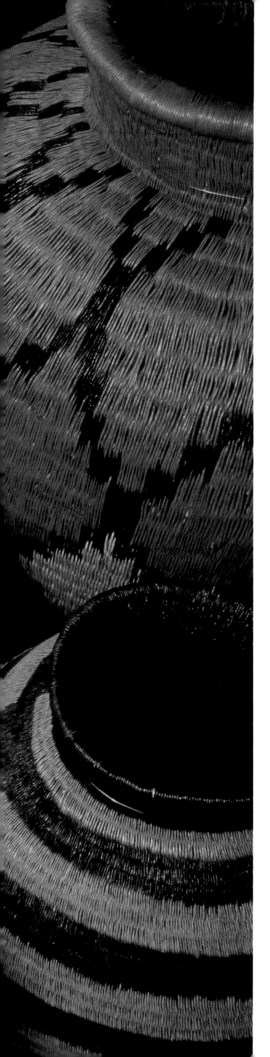

MATERIALS

FAR LEFT: *Werregué palm-fibre baskets, Colombia.*
LEFT: *Bamboo rice basket, Nepal.*
BELOW, LEFT: *Palm frond bowl, St Lucia.*
BELOW, RIGHT: *Coiled grass Tutsi baskets, Rwanda.*

MATERIALS

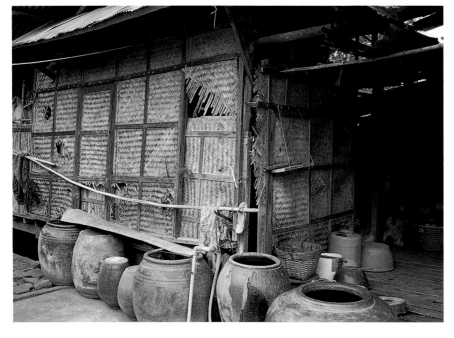

ABOVE, LEFT: *Phormium tenax, or harakeke as the Maoris call it, growing in New Zealand. It is the Maoris' most prized material.*
LEFT: *Bamboo grove in Thailand.*
ABOVE: *A house with walls of plaited bamboo in Bang Kaew, a fishing village in southern Thailand.*
ABOVE, RIGHT: *Owen Jones trimming oak spars on a shave horse to make Cumberland swill baskets, England.*
BELOW: *In the Japanese village of Kiryu, a basketmaker splits lengths of bamboo into thin strips.*

OUR planet is made up of a great diversity of climatic and topographical regions, wet or dry, cold or hot, flat or mountainous, each of which is host to plants that have evolved in order to survive there. As all crafts were developed by early peoples using the materials they had to hand, basketmaking materials and techniques vary considerably from one region to another.

LOCAL MATERIALS

IN the vast forests that once covered the north of America, Europe and Asia, the most readily available materials were the bark, twigs, wood and roots of trees. Baskets of birch bark or spruce roots can be made by gathering wild materials, but where woodland is cultivated and coppiced, the whippy stems of trees such as willow are used in the manufacture of stake and strand baskets.

In hot, wet regions such as Southeast Asia the jungles and forests are a rich source of fast-growing plants – bamboo and rattan, for instance – and these are employed, plaited or interlaced in a number of ways to provide many of the daily needs of the inhabitants, from burden baskets to fishtraps, from sleeping mats to musical instruments.

Prairies and savannahs sustain a vast amount of grass, but few trees. In such regions as the grasslands of southern Africa, the great majority of baskets are made from bundles of coiled and stitched grass. In contrast, wetlands produce reeds and rushes, deserts are home to fibrous succulents such as the yucca and agave, the tropics are ideal for palms, while agricultural land provides a great abundance of straw.

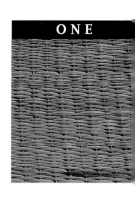

TRADE AND INDUSTRIALIZATION

THE development of global transport and trade has led to many changes to tradition. The British, for instance, introduced willow cultivation into Kashmir in the nineteenth century to meet their colonial needs. Today, the most popular material of all is rattan, which is exported in great quantities from the Philippines and Indonesia to all over the Western world.

Industrialization has meant the loss of many natural habitats and the plants, often used for making baskets, that lived there. It has also produced a new material – plastic.

ABOVE, LEFT: *Making a stake and strand rattan basket in Accra, Ghana. Rattan is perhaps the most widely used basketmaking material of all.*
ABOVE, RIGHT: *Plaiting coconut frond in Samoa, where it is used for bags, mats and even wall panels.*
RIGHT: *Coconut plantations yield fronds, leaf ribs, coir and trunk fibres which can all be used for basketmaking.*
BELOW, RIGHT: *A yucca tree growing in the USA's arid Southwest.*

BELOW: *Bamboo baskets for sale on the Indonesian island of Lombok. The ones at the front are hex-weave cages for fighting cocks and chickens.*
RIGHT: *Harvesting agave leaves in Mexico's Yucatán peninsula to make sisal.*

BAMBOO

BAMBOOS grow naturally in the temperate and tropical zones of every continent except Europe and Antarctica. Their high lignin content makes them tough and resilient, endowing the outer surface with a golden sheen. The hollow culms or stems are reinforced at the nodes, enabling them to grow long without snapping. There are hundreds of different species, ranging from dwarves less than half a metre (1 ft) high to giants that have been recorded as being as high as 54 metres (180 ft). One particularly vigorous bamboo can grow well over a metre (4 ft) in a single day!

Bamboo is probably the most versatile and useful of all plants. The diverse list of its uses includes scaffolding, water pipes, weapons, musical instruments, boats, furniture, acupuncture needles, bridges, umbrellas, the filament of Edison's first light bulb – and, of course, baskets. For basketry, the culms must be split into skeins or splints.

This tough stake and strand bamboo basket from Taiwan has been reinforced with a broader strip of bent bamboo. It has many different uses.

Double-layered conical hat plaited from strips of split bamboo. Hats like this are found all over Southeast Asia.

Cultivation

BAMBOOS flower and produce seed like grasses, but they are normally propagated by taking cuttings from their rhizomes. As the rhizome becomes established, it sends up new culms each year; these gradually spread to produce a clump or grove. After three years, culms are harvested by cutting them off above the second node.

Preparation

IF the culms are intended for basketry, they must be sawn into convenient lengths and split lengthwise. This can be accomplished with a sharp machete or a splitter with several blades. For fine work these splints may be split several times to provide pieces of the required width. The pithy inner culm is then removed to leave the harder outer layers, which can be split into finer layers with further tangential cuts. The toughest layer of all is the shiny outer strip.

THE CH'AN (ZEN) PATRIARCH HUI-NENG CUTTING BAMBOO, AFTER A THIRTEENTH-CENTURY PAINTING

Distribution and uses

IN India, Indochina, China and Japan baskets are an indispensable part of daily life and they are most often manufactured from bamboo. Finely split, flexible skeins are used to make anything from hats to lunch boxes, while thick strips are used in the construction of large, sometimes crude, baskets for heavy goods. Basketry techniques are also employed to build fences, houses and even bridges from interlaced, large splints or unsplit culms.

LEFT: *Made from very finely split bamboo by the Ka'chin people of northern Myanmar (Burma), this cage or trap is only 10 cm (4 in.) long.*
RIGHT: *A Balinese basket with bands of tight weaving and openwork. The rim is a broad band of bamboo.*
BELOW, LEFT: *Cambodian basket formed by a combination of plaiting and stake and strand. (diameter x height: 37 x 28 cm, 14½ x 11 in.)*
INSET: *This fence in Cha-Am, southern Thailand, is made from lengths of coarsely split bamboo.*

21

RATTAN

ATTAN, a native of Indochina, the Philippines and the Pacific, is a tropical climbing palm and probably the most popular basketmaking material of all. Using long thorns on its vine-like stems, it climbs up other jungle plants and can reach lengths in excess of 150 metres (490 ft), but is never more than a few centimetres thick. Different parts of the plant are used for a variety of purposes and processed cane is now exported all around the world for basketmaking.

Whole cane

THE thorny bark must be stripped away to reveal the shiny layer beneath. Thinner stems may be used in this state to construct baskets that bear a passing resemblance to willow work, but you can tell the difference by the presence of conspicuous nodes at intervals on the stems of rattan, but not willow. During the nineteenth century rattan replaced willow in the construction of baskets used by English fishermen for trapping, containing and transporting wet seafood.

ABOVE: *Coiled rattan basket from Bangladesh; the coils are secured with bamboo nails.*

Thicker stems can be heated or steamed and bent into shapes that they will retain. These are bound or nailed together to make tough, but light, furniture.

Split cane

T HE tough, shiny inner bark can be separated from the pithy centre and split into strips which, in terms of colour and sheen, look very like split bamboo. These strips are used locally for making a diverse selection of baskets, but huge quantities are now exported for use in weaving chair seating.

Centre cane

T HE core of the rattan plant is made up of a pliant substance which is split into various thicknesses and smoothed. Known as centre, pulp or pith cane, or reed, this flexible material, available in handy lengths of consistent thickness, is ideal for basketmaking and is exported all over the world.

Although rattan centre cane lacks the beauty of willow, having a dull, light colour and no sheen, it is very easy to use and was once favoured by beginners, amateurs and professional blind basketmakers. It is frequently used today in the manufacture of stylish garden or conservatory furniture.

OPPOSITE, BELOW: *Ambong bags, made from twill-plaited split rattan by the Penan of Sarawak, used to carry personal belongings on journeys.*
OPPOSITE, INSET: *Kayan men, from Sarawak, splitting rattan. Rattan is used in at least half the crafts practised in Borneo and Kalimantan.*
TOP, LEFT: *Back pack made from twill-plaited rattan by the Ifugao or Bontoc, who live in the hills of northern Luzon in the Philippines.*
ABOVE: *A European-style frame basket made from whole cane.*
ABOVE, RIGHT: *A smoke-blackened rod-coiled basket from the Indonesian island of Lombok. Similar baskets are used for storing cooked rice all over Southeast Asia.*
RIGHT: *Group of small rod-coiled baskets from Lombok (8 cm, 3 in. high). Baskets like these made from rattan rods are very strong.*

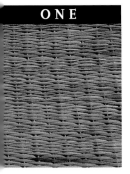

WITHIES AND WANDS

THE pliant shoots of deciduous, hardwood trees and shrubs such as hazel, cotton-wood and willow are ideal for basketmaking. Many societies once burned trees to stimulate fresh growth and ensure a supply of young straight shoots of a suitable length. However, as first documented by Pliny the Elder (AD 23–79), by the 1st century AD the more controlled woodland industry of coppicing deciduous trees had developed.

Coppicing

CUTTINGS about 30 cm (12 in.) long are taken from a hardwood tree such as willow (*Salix* species) or hazel (*Coryllus avellana*) and are planted and left to root. After a few years all growth is cut back to a stump or 'stool' near the ground to stimulate growth. A number of shoots will sprout from the stool and should reach a height of around 2 metres (6½ ft) before they are harvested each autumn.

Willow

MANY trees and shrubs can be coppiced, but willow wands, popularly known as osiers or withies, are the supreme basketmaking material in Europe, and are cultivated in 'beds' or 'garths'. The many different varieties of the *Salix* family offer a choice of strength, flexibility and colour. Willow is an incredibly vigorous plant and a planted cutting is almost guaranteed to sprout.

Processing

FRESHLY cut willow rods, heavy with sap and called 'greens', may be used without processing to make cheap baskets such as those often employed by florists.

When dried and used with the bark intact, rods are referred to as 'browns' and are used in the construction of tough items, for instance, log baskets.

Rods kept standing in a few inches of water until April, when the sap begins to rise, can be easily stripped of their bark by pulling them through a metal 'brake'. This produces attractive 'white' rods suitable for quality basketry. 'Buffs' are coloured by boiling them before stripping which allows the natural tannins in the bark to dye the rods a chestnut brown. Like many other materials, willow stored dry must be soaked to soften it before basketmaking commences.

Skeins

PEELED rods can be split lengthwise into three or more pieces by using a cleave to produce 'skeins'. Once trimmed, these are ideal for fine, light or delicate basketmaking.

ABOVE, LEFT: *Coppiced hazel, Kent, England.*
LEFT: *Coppiced willow, Cambridgeshire, England.*
TOP RIGHT: *Twined Apache water jar awaiting a coat of piñon pitch to make it waterproof; made by Charlene Lupe from sumac shoots.*
RIGHT, CENTRE: *Drying stripped willow in Germany, early twentieth century.*
RIGHT: *Latvian basket made with a whole-willow rod foundation stitched with skeined willow.*

ABOVE: *A willow mat made from skeined willow; probably French. Skeins can be produced by hand, but machinery was developed in Germany which saved time and money.*

LEFT: *This French stake and strand basket in the form of a bottle was constructed from tightly woven willow skeins. Much particularly fine skeined work has been produced in northeast France, Belgium and the Netherlands.*

BELOW: *White willow platter made to a traditional Polish design by English basketmaker Mary Butcher.*

SPLIT WOOD

HARDWOOD, deciduous trees, such as oak, ash and sweet chestnut, that do not produce pliant shoots suitable for basketmaking can be split into flexible slats known, according to region, as splints, spells, spelks or spale. Work of this kind has most often been carried out by craftsmen living in or near the woodland where the trees were felled.

Splitting

NORTH American tribes, such as the Menominee of Wisconsin, used splints in their baskets. They obtained the splints by hitting a branch with a mallet until the fibres split apart along the growth rings.

In Europe, the trunks of felled trees are first quartered lengthwise and then

BELOW: *A basket of split chestnut acquired in eastern England. In Sweden similar baskets are made from juniper.*
BELOW, INSET: *Splitting wood with a blade in the hunting forest of Sologne in France.*
RIGHT: *Slovak back pack of riven hazel.*

heated, usually by boiling or steaming. The fire is traditionally stoked with the waste materials from previous work. Heating opens up the fibres of the wood so that it can then be easily riven (split) with a heavy metal blade.

Shaping

ONCE the slats have been cut into suitable lengths, they are then clamped in a wooden vice called a horse which the craftsman sits astride. He then pares them down to the thickness and width that he requires for a particular basket, using a drawknife. Normally this means shaving both ends so that they taper to allow for the curvature of the basket.

Uses and distribution

TOUGH baskets are made from wooden slats all over the northern hemisphere. Most often they are frame baskets built up on or around a frame of spars bent from a wood such as hazel or ash. In the English Lake District swill baskets of interlaced oak are still made in a number of traditional shapes and sizes for use as horse panniers, shopping baskets or charcoal burners' scuttles. The Sussex trug, a garden basket of split oak or cricket bat willow nailed to a frame of ash or

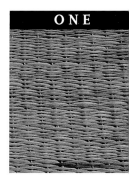

chestnut, was not invented until the 1850s, but gained instant celebrity after Queen Victoria bought several at the Great Exhibition of 1851.

In many parts of northern Europe thin splints or strips of veneer have been used to make rectangular punnets or 'chips' for gathering soft fruit and vegetables, although these have, by and large, been superseded by factory-made cardboard boxes. A more sophisticated rectangular version is a painted basket from Gästrikland in Sweden.

In North America splint baskets were made by indigenous peoples and also by European colonists. Split oak features in many of the baskets made in the Appalachian Mountains.

ABOVE: *Polish punnet or 'chip' constructed from plaited strips of pine veneer secured with staples. Baskets like this have been superseded by cardboard boxes.*
LEFT: *A Cumberland swill made by Owen Jones. This basket from the English Lake District is made from riven oak on a hazel frame.*
LEFT, INSET: *A woman from Austria selling apples on the streets of Vienna. She is holding a frame basket made from split wood.*

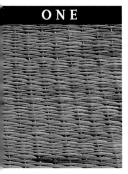

BARK

IN many contexts bark is a waste material, but resourceful basketmakers around the world have found the bark of particular trees and shrubs to be of great value.

Bark sheets

UNDER the outer skin of trees such as elm and birch is a layer that can be peeled away in a sheet. The Native Americans of the great forests of North America, in particular, exploited these sheets in the construction of many things, from houses to canoes. Smaller bark containers were used to perform daily chores, including winnowing wild rice, collecting maple syrup or carrying water. To make these containers, sheets of bark were cut to size, softened with heat and then bent into shape. They were held in place with stitching, or by pinning, or glueing with gum.

Pots and boxes like these were often embellished. The Chippewa and Ojibway specialized in the use of porcupine quills, the Huron and Iroquois in moosehair and the Cree in split goose quills. Eastern tribes such as the Penobscot often created patterns by scraping away layers of bark to reveal the different colours beneath.

TOP: *Salt pot made in Finland by Santeri Jekkonen from plaited birch bark strips.*
LEFT: *A coiled basket from Mali. The coils are of grass and bark stitched with strips of bark.*

Bark sheet strips

IN Norway, Finland, northern Russia and the Baltic states, country naturally thickly forested with birch trees, birch bark is cut into strips a few centimetres wide and interlaced to construct double-layered baskets. Containers made in this way are used for anything from salt to coins, as well as for carrying produce or shopping. Devoid of pattern, they are rendered attractive by the golden hue of the naturally coloured bark.

Fibrous bark

THE bark of some trees such as the cedar is stringy and can be shredded and twisted into pliant strands. This was the chosen material of tribes of the American Northwest such as the Makah of Washington State and Nuu-chah-nulth (Nootka) of Vancouver Island who still produce delicately patterned, twined cedar bark bowls and hats. In Africa, the Senufo of the Ivory Coast also use twined baobab bark in the construction of their hats and other objects such as baskets and domestic utensils.

Outer bark

STRIPS of bark have been used in West Africa, Europe and North America to add colour to baskets. In the American Northwest, for example, cherry bark was often used for imbricated patterns. In Mali baskets are also traditionally stitched with bark, although since the 1970s environmental changes have made it necessary to substitute strips of rice sack for bark.

ABOVE: Willow and willow bark basket made by a French fisherman. Baskets like this are traditionally made by fishermen every few years for their own use as their old ones need replacing.
RIGHT: A plaited birch bark container from Karelia, just south of the Arctic circle, straddling the borders of Russia and Finland.
BELOW: Folded birch bark baskets. The one on the left, from Archangel, Russia, is for collecting birch sap. The two on the right were made by Alaskan Eskimos.

ROOTS

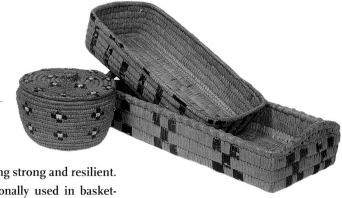

ROOTS can be surprisingly long and flexible, as well as being strong and resilient. The roots of deciduous trees such as birch are occasionally used in basket-making, but the roots of conifers, in particular spruce, are much more widely exploited.

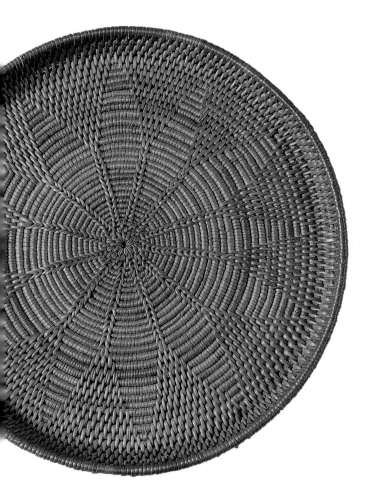

Conifer roots

THE finer roots of the spruce, *Picea abies*, may reach 13 metres (42½ ft) in length. They are tough, but can be split easily into pliant skeins that have a very pleasing honey colour. Conifer root is used for basketmaking in Scandinavia and for frame baskets around the Baltic, where it is employed or treated in much the same way as skeined willow.

In the west of the USA and Canada, notably among the Salishan peoples of the Thompson River, sturdy, rectangular storage baskets and cradles of coiled spruce roots are often decorated with a superimposed textured layer worked with the imbrication technique. On the northwestern coast finely split spruce root is used by the Kwakiutl and Haida to construct high-crowned hats with a twining technique, incorporating very fine raised twill patterns. Some of these hats are further embellished with painted animal designs.

Sedge roots

THE indigenous peoples of northern California excelled in making twined or coiled baskets used in processing staple foods such as acorns. Some of these employ conifer root as foundations or stitching, while others use the roots of sedge. Sedges must be cultivated in as loose and stonefree a soil as can be achieved to ensure that the rhizomes will grow as straight and long as possible. Pomo baskets, the most elaborate, are decorated with shells, beads and even red woodpecker feathers.

Other roots

THE most famous of all Native American basketmakers was probably Datsolalee (1831–1926), a Washo from Nevada. Her

exquisite coiled willow baskets were much sought after by white collectors during her lifetime. They were decorated with delicate red and black motifs stitched with redbud bark and fern root. The red pattern sections in baskets made by Native Americans in the arid country of New Mexico, Arizona and Sonora were achieved with the roots of the banana yucca, *Yucca arizonica*, also known as Spanish dagger because of its spiky leaves.

In the Scottish Orkney Islands heather roots were once used in the construction of a fish creel called a *cassie*.

TOP: *A group of imbricated spruce-root baskets made by Salish speakers from the Thompson River in the interior of British Columbia, Canada.*
ABOVE, LEFT: *Coiled tray, with decorative stitching, made in Latvia from split pine root.*
BELOW, LEFT: *Karok basketmaker twining baskets from sedge roots. Photographed on the Hupa Reservation, northwestern California, by John Daggett in 1896.*
ABOVE: *Salish spruce-root basket. Imbricated patterns were worked over the spruce-root foundation in bleached grass or cherry bark.*
OPPOSITE: *A watertight Polish basket made by Stanislaw Kumanrowicz. Pine root has been woven around a juniper frame.*
OPPOSITE, INSET: *Joseppa Beatty, a Pomo basketmaker from California, making a basket with coils of sedge root.*

GRASSES

G RASSES are slender plants that send up undivided, hollow stems from creeping roots. Long thin leaves grow alternately up the stems which produce light feathery flower panicles with tiny seeds. Generally, it is the stems that are used in basketmaking. Although most grasses are small and slender, some species can grow to over one metre (3 ft) in height and are used to construct surprisingly rigid structures.

ABOVE: *Baskets of coiled sweetgrass bundles made around 1890 by Chippewa people from the Canadian side of the Great Lakes. Fragrant sweetgrass was used in many Native American shamanic rituals. The lids are made of birch bark decorated with porcupine quills.*

BELOW: *Bundle-coiled Moroccan mat of esparto grass. Mats and bowls are also made using dyed esparto grass to create bold patterns.*

Distribution

THE grass family contains many species and different varieties have adapted to virtually every conceivable habitat and are to be found in all corners of the globe. In some regions, such as the savannahs of Africa, the Prairies of North America and the Pampas of South America, oceans of grass once stretched for hundreds of miles, providing grazing for many herbivores. This was ideal country for hunter-gatherer societies, but provided no wood for basketry. Out of necessity, the only materials available were adapted and used in the construction of baskets.

Techniques

GRASS may look too fragile to be used to make a basket, but several techniques have been developed that exploit its qualities to the full. A bundle of grass has mass and flexibility, and therefore the walls of baskets can be made by coiling and stitching bundles together. One fine example is the sweetgrass basket made by the tribes of the North American Plains which has the bonus of a pleasant smell.

Grass stems can also be twisted without breaking which makes them a suitable material for twined basketry. In the sub-Sahara, where there are few materials available, grass twining has become a refined art among peoples such as the Fulani of Mali and Niger.

Large grasses

ONE tall specimen, reaching 70–100 cm (27–39 in.) in height, is esparto grass, *Stipa tenacissima*, a native of north-west Africa and southern Spain. It may be used as found or beaten flat to make bags, baskets and mats.

In Tripura and Manipura, northeast India, one commonly made item of furniture is the *mudah*, a stool constructed from bamboo stems. A similar stool, the *mura*, is made in Haryana state, but owing to difficulties in obtaining suitable cane, a version is now made from local *jhunda* grass bound together with twine.

ABOVE: *A twined basket of brightly dyed savannah grass from the Bolgatang district of northern Ghana, where the same materials and technique are used to make many other items, including hats and fans.*

LEFT: *Large bundle-coiled grass basket made by the Tutsi of Burundi. This basket is 41 cm (16 in.) high, but others, virtually identical visually, reach only 10 cm (4 in.) and may be constructed from silky bundles no thicker than one or two millimetres.*

BELOW: *Twined grass basket, from Tanzania, of a type common in East Africa.*

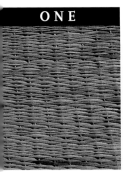

REEDS AND SEDGES

Rᴇᴇᴅꜱ are tall, hollow-stemmed members of the genera *Phragmites* or *Arundo* which grow in swamps, marshes and freshwater where they often reach heights of 250 cm (8 ft) or more. Sedges belong to the *Carex* or *Cyperaceae* family and, although some are grassy plants only a foot or so high, others grow tall and are used in the same way as reeds. In the USA the term 'reed' means rattan.

Cultivation and preparation

Rᴇᴇᴅꜱ and sedges are grown in large beds in soggy or flooded lowland. Harvesting takes place in the summer between mid-June and August when the stems are cut as low as possible with a sharp hook. The stems are laid on dry ground and allowed to dry before being tied into bundles or 'bolts'. They are then stored in a cool place or under tarpaulins until required.

Distribution and uses

Rᴇᴇᴅꜱ are used to make mats and baskets in any part of the world where they can be found growing in slow-moving water, marshes or swamps.

In Britain the best reed is *Phragmites communis* which has been used for centuries to thatch roofs. Before the invention of roofing felt, a large mat or 'fleekin', which acted as a base layer, was woven from bundles of reed 5 cm (2 in.) thick. The same reeds are cultivated in Turkey for export and domestic use. They are employed to make shallow, bundle-coiled dishes and large mats on which freshly baked bread is stored. In Sarawak, bemban, *Donax grandis* or *arundostratum*, is used in basketry as a substitute for rattan or bamboo. *Arundo donax*, another bamboo-like reed, is widely used in Greece and Turkey.

Sedges absorb dye well, a quality exploited in Malaysia and Madagascar in the weaving of colourful mats and bags.

In Egypt papyrus, *Cyperus papyrus*, was used in ancient times for basketry, for making paper and was tied into huge bundles to make boats. It is still employed in Rwanda and Uganda for patterning large *inkangara* baskets.

LᴇꜰT: *Reeds from Norfolk, England, on the left, and from Turkey, on the right.*
Rɪɢʜᴛ: *An* Arundo donax *basket made on the Greek island of Lemnos.*
Bᴇʟᴏᴡ: *Malagasy basket of plaited* zozoro *sedge.*

ABOVE: *Coiled reed basket with spaced stitching, acquired near Alanya, Turkey.*
LEFT: *Early twentieth-century Tutsi basket from Rwanda; bundle-coiled grasses with black decoration worked in dyed papyrus (1 m, 3 ft high).*
RIGHT: Phragmites communis *growing in Cambridgeshire, England.*
BELOW: *A typical twill-plaited Cherokee basket from the southeast of the USA. Cherokee and Chitimacha baskets are normally made from river cane,* Arundinaria tecta.

In Colombia the ever-popular broad-brimmed *vueltiao* hat is made from coils of geometrically patterned braids of black and white arrow reed.

Seagrass

SEAGRASS is a member of the *Carex* family found growing in Italy, Switzerland and the Camargue in southern France. It is easily obtainable as a twisted cord and makes an ideal chair-seating fibre since it is tough and pliable. In former times it was also used in the highlands around Zürich, Switzerland, for making sewing and harvest baskets.

RUSHES

THERE was a time in medieval Europe when the height of luxury was the strewing of fresh rushes on the floor. Their pithy softness made them pleasant to walk on and their fresh smell counteracted, to some extent, the filth and odours of sweat and smoke. These same characteristics have made rushes a useful material for mats and baskets right up to the present day.

Types of rush

POND rushes, members of the *Scirpus* species, can grow up to 4 m (13 ft) tall and make ideal weaving materials. Easily confused with these, and also widely exploited, are cattails. The tallest, the reed mace, *Typha latifolia*, with its thick flower spike, is often incorrectly referred to as 'bulrush', a term correctly applied to *Scirpus lacustris*. The smaller plants of the *Juncus* species have thinner stems, also pithy, and may be used for finer work such as the baskets of the Californian Chumash.

LEFT: *A Pima basket, from southern Arizona, made to be sold, and not for home use. It is constructed with bundles of split cattails stitched with willow (16 cm, 6 in. high).*

ABOVE: *In Europe many rush baskets were once plaited over a mould such as a shoe box or, in this case, a flowerpot.*

BELOW: *Most baskets made by the Pima for their own use, like this* olla *(about 41 cm, 16 in. high), are urn, dish or bowl shaped.*

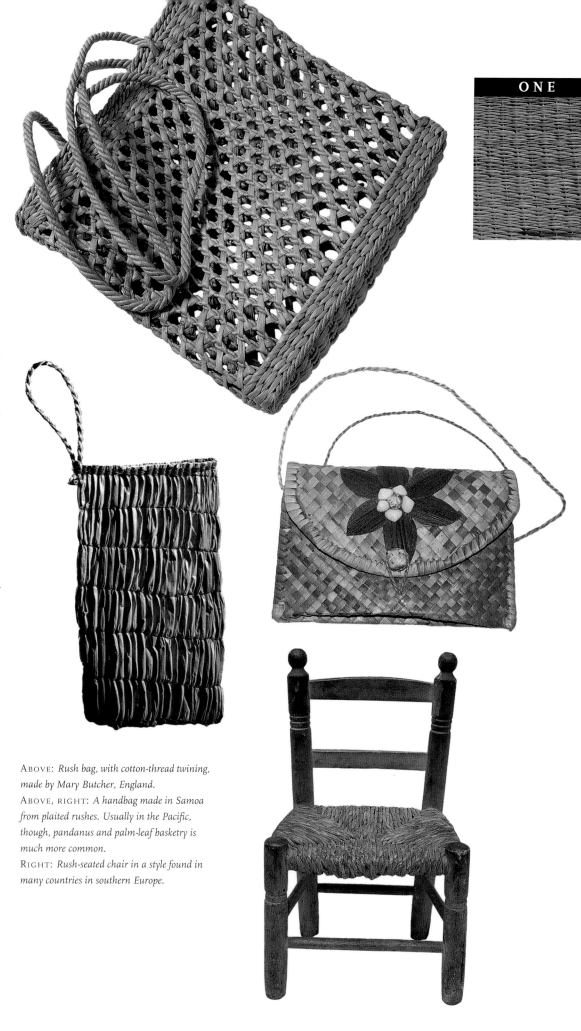

RIGHT: *A rush shopping bag of unknown origin. The borders are twined for strength, but the bulk of the bag has an unusual hexagonal weave with twisted warps.*

Cultivation

RUSHES, like reeds, grow in marshes and slow-moving water. However, the stems are not hollow, but filled with spongy vesicles which gives items made from them a soft, springy quality. Rushes are cut in mid-summer, often from a boat. The cut stems are laid to dry on the river bank or on wooden racks and are then stored in a cool, dark place until needed. Before they can be used, rushes must be sprinkled with water and allowed to stand for several hours so they become soft and pliable.

Distribution and uses

RUSHES are fibrous and flexible when damp so they can be plaited, twined or coiled and are used in the construction of many baskets, mats and other structures, including comfortable shoes and hats. Rush baskets are often made over a mould.

The bulrush, *Scirpus lacustris*, is the most commonly used rush in Europe where it is employed most often for chair seating and bags. In Turkey rush mats are the traditional underlay for flatweave kilim rugs.

The 'reed' boats, or *totora*, used on Lake Titicaca in South America are made from a rush, *Scirpus totora*, which is also used in the construction of houses. In Ecuador, although the supply of *totora* is dwindling, it is still used for weaving mats to cover floors and walls.

Native Americans of the Great Lakes regions used cattails to weave mats, while in the Southwest they were employed for the foundations of coiled baskets.

ABOVE: *Rush bag, with cotton-thread twining, made by Mary Butcher, England.*
ABOVE, RIGHT: *A handbag made in Samoa from plaited rushes. Usually in the Pacific, though, pandanus and palm-leaf basketry is much more common.*
RIGHT: *Rush-seated chair in a style found in many countries in southern Europe.*

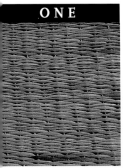

STRAW

GRAIN of one kind or another – rice, barley, wheat, millet – is the staple food of many sedentary, agriculture-based societies. The grains grow at the top of long, hollow stalks which, when dry, are known as straw. Basketry is one of the many uses to which this waste product is put. Straw basketry was once common in Italy, Switzerland, France, the Former Yugoslavia, Austria and Britain.

Harvest rituals

SUPERSTITIONS surrounding the Spirit of the Corn abound worldwide, but the corn 'dolly' probably originated in the harvest sacrifices of Asia Minor. As the harvest progresses, the Spirit retreats into a smaller and smaller place until finally he or she is trapped in the last uncut sheaf. Here he is either captured or ritually slaughtered. In England he was imprisoned in a cage made from the twisted straws of the last sheaf. This artform has been kept alive to this day in the construction of corn 'dollies', the imagery of which varies from one county to another. Similar figures are also made in many other parts of Europe and also in Mexico. For this task, only the section of stem above the top leaf node is used.

Twining

IN the Shetland Islands to the far north of Scotland oat straw is one of the few available materials. By twisting it into ropes and binding them together with twining, the islanders have developed the 'kishie', an all-purpose basket predominantly used for carrying peat. Dried dock stalks may also be used.

ABOVE: Japanese decoration depicting the rice harvest

ABOVE: English corn dolly. This is a traditional Suffolk design showing a horseshoe and a carter's whip.
ABOVE, RIGHT: Box from Chile made with natural and dyed straw. The construction is very similar to that of corn dollies.
BELOW: Chinese straw tray.

Coiled straw

STRAW can be bundled up, twisted and sewn into coiled containers. This process has been used in the manufacture of shopping baskets, beehives (skeps) and log baskets. It is sometimes called 'lipwork' as it was often used in the construction of sowing baskets, or 'seed lips' as they are also known. In Syria wheatstraw is dyed and employed for the stitching of colourful mats on which food is served.

Straw braids

PLAITED into braids, straw acquires greater strength, but remains flexible. This makes it ideal for bending into coiled millinery. Many sewing baskets of interlaced straw braids were made during Edwardian times at the beginning of the twentieth century for the British colonial market. Today, they are still constructed in China, using dyed rice straw.

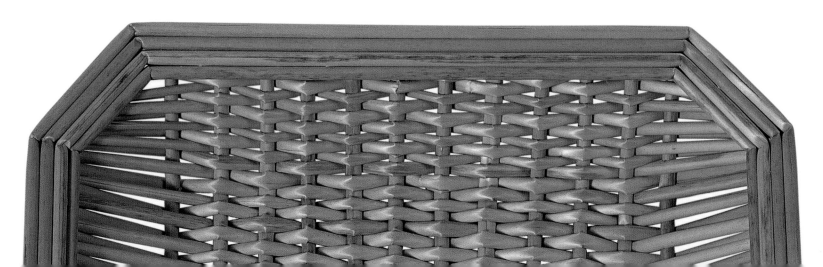

LEFT: *Ian Beaty, a Cambridgeshire beekeeper, making a bee skep from coiled rye straw.*
BELOW: *A lipwork basket from Romney Marsh, in the English county of Kent. It is made from bundles of wheat straw stitched with tarred string.*
BELOW, INSET: *Shetland women transporting produce packed into oat-straw kishies to market.*

PALMS

T HE Natural Order *Palmaceae* is a large family of monocotyledonous trees and shrubs that mainly grow in tropical and subtropical regions of the world. They normally have a tall trunk that branches at the top into a head of pinnate or palmate leaves. Many palms, such as coconuts and dates, are cultivated for their fruits and their leaves, which are used in basketmaking.

Preparation

T HE natural form of a palm leaf – leaflets branching off a spine – has been exploited in many places as the starting-point for simple basketry. By using the leaf intact and interlacing the leaflets, it is possible to make simple hats, mats and building panels, or quite sophisticated bags and variations as are found all over the Caribbean and the Pacific.

Cutting the leaves allows a greater degree of manipulation and so a wide variety of baskets can be made. The leaflets must be split off the central spine and slit into narrow strips. This can be accomplished by pulling them through a set of narrow, closely spaced blades. The strips are then dried before being stored or sold and are often then bleached or dyed. Before use, they must be dampened to soften them.

Uses

P ALM strips are easy to manipulate and may be employed in several ways. They may be plaited as, for instance, in hats from northern Bali, Tarahumara Indian baskets from Mexico, or mats made since time immemorial in Egypt. They may be plaited and sewn in coils as straw often is to make hats. They may also be employed for both the bundles and the stitching of coiled baskets. One superlative example of this is the basketry of the Cholo Indians who live in the Chocó of Colombia. They make coiled baskets, which are capable of holding water, from the leaves of the *werregué* palm dyed in reds, browns and blacks. These baskets are so finely stitched that from a distance they could be mistaken for pottery.

Other parts of the palm

T HE spathe (the section of stem that connects the leaf to the trunk of the palm) is used in some communities to reinforce carrying baskets. In the Philippines the ribs are split from the leaflets of coconut palms and woven into stiff openwork baskets. The hairy coir peeled off the coconut fruit may also be used in the making of rope, mats and containers.

ABOVE: DATE PALM, AFTER A PAINTING IN THE TOMB OF SENNEDJEM, A TOMB WORKER, DEIR EL-MEDINA, LUXOR, EGYPT, 19TH DYNASTY, C. 1200 BC

TOP: *Japanese farmer's rain hat made with fibres from a palm trunk.*
ABOVE: *Coiled Zulu pot stitched with strips of ilala palm. Many of these pots are woven tightly enough to hold water.*
RIGHT: *Hawaiian bowls, each constructed from a single coconut frond.*

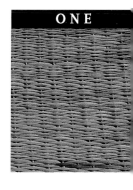

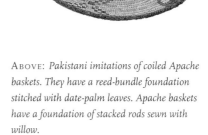

ABOVE: *A bag plaited from a single frond made in Guyana, South America; similar to many made on Pacific islands.*

LEFT: *Stripping the ribs from coconut fronds in southern Thailand.*

BELOW: *Set of Tarahumara baskets of plaited palm strips, from Chihuahua, Mexico.*

ABOVE: *Pakistani imitations of coiled Apache baskets. They have a reed-bundle foundation stitched with date-palm leaves. Apache baskets have a foundation of stacked rods sewn with willow.*

PANDANUS

In Hawaii, they say that when Madam Pele, the volcano goddess, first landed, her canoe became entangled in the roots of the pandanus. In her rage she tore the tree to shreds and cast the pieces in all directions. Wherever they landed they took root and have provided the islanders with basketmaking materials ever since.

The word 'pandanus' is derived from the Malay word *pandan* – the plant is common in the Malay archipelago. Its more prosaic English name is the 'screw-pine'. The various species all have vicious thorns on the spines and sides of the leaves. Once prepared, pandanus fibres are very flexible, bearing a strong resemblance to palm fibre, and are used to make fine, delicate objects.

Preparation

COLLECTING pandanus leaves is an unpleasant task because of the thorns. The leaves must be split to remove the thick spine and sharp edges, and dried in the sun or over a fire to soften them. They are then cut into narrow strips in the same way as palm leaves by pulling them through a comb with sharp blades for teeth. The strips are soaked and rinsed several times to remove the sap and then bleached in the sun.

Pandanus fibres are very absorbent and easy to dye. Many modern products exploit the convenience of synthetic dyes for their vibrant colours.

BELOW: Tutup *foodcovers, from Sibutu Island, south Philippines, constructed from dyed pandanus leaves. (Larger: 23 cm, 9 in. high)*

Distribution

IF the legend is true, then Madam Pele must have had a strong arm because pandanus baskets are made in locations as far flung as Sri Lanka and Ecuador.

In Indonesia and Malaysia pandanus is most often used for plaiting mats. Particularly fine mats are woven in the Malaysian state of Sabah, the southern provinces of Thailand, Terengganu in Malaya and Aceh in Sumatra.

A variety of basketwork is carried out in Australia, including the construction of the Aborigines' all-purpose carrier, the

ABOVE: *Soft, double-layered, finely plaited pandanus mats from Aceh, Sumatra. (46 x 46 cm, 18 x 18 in.) Fine pandanus mats are also produced in Malaya, southern Thailand and the Philippines.*

OPPOSITE, TOP: *This photograph of pandanus growing in northern Australia clearly shows why it is known as the 'screw-pine'.*
OPPOSITE, CENTRE: *Nesting wallets from Sri Lanka plaited from thin strips of pandanus. (Largest wallet: 16 x 26 cm, 6 x 10 in.)*

dilly bag. These may be twined or inter-looped and are often made from pandanus.

In Hawaii and Polynesia pandanus is one of the main basketmaking materials and is used to make anything from sails to headbands.

In Latin America pandanus fibres are used for panama hats. Coiled baskets of pandanus are also made by the Chocó Indians who live in the Darien area of Panama. The fibres are dyed with mud and bark and woven into pre-Colombian, totemic designs of animals, birds and insects.

LEFT: *Plaited pandanus baskets from Ecuador. (12 x 7 cm, 5 x 3 in.)*
ABOVE: *A 'mad weave' – tightly woven hex weave – pandanus basket made by Malays in south Thailand. (8 cm, 3 in. high)*

LEAF FIBRES

Mᴀɴʏ plants produce leaves that are long and strong enough to be used in basketmaking with very little processing. Others may be stripped down into fibres fine enough to sew with or to twist into cords.

New Zealand flax

Tᴏ the Maoris, the fibre par excellence has always been New Zealand flax, *Phormium tenax*, which they call *harakeke*. It is used to make mats, canoe sails, decorative wall hangings and the *kete* basket, which has now become a symbol of tribal identity. Slit into fine strips, phormium is plaited into baskets, but it may also be twisted into yarn for use in the manufacture of netting and twined cloaks.

Yucca

Iɴ the arid regions in the Southwest of the USA and Mexico various species of yucca are used for the same purposes as flax. Baskets and sandals were made from yucca by the Anasazi who lived in the region hundreds of years ago. It is still used by their descendants and successors to make fine coiled and plaited trays, sifters, plaques and baskets.

Sisal

Oʀɪɢɪɴᴀʟʟʏ from the New World, *Agave sisalana* was introduced to Europe by the Spanish who recognized its potential. Since then it has been cultivated in many places, including tropical Africa. It is a large succulent whose fleshy leaves are held together with long stringy fibres that, once separated from the pulp, are ideal for twisting into coarse, but strong, cord. One example of their use is for the bulbous, twined *kiondo* bags made in Kenya which are now exported in large quantities to Europe.

Raffia

Tʜᴇ raffia palm, *Raphia taedigera*, grows in Central Africa and Madagascar. The leaves may reach 15 metres (49 ft) in

Aʙᴏᴠᴇ: *A Maori* kete *made from plaited* Phormium tenax. *Skilled weavers are able to produce a whole range of twilled patterns in two colours.*

Aʙᴏᴠᴇ, ʀɪɢʜᴛ: *Loading* Phormium tenax *to be taken to a flax mill in New Zealand. The Maoris prefer to cut by hand, so they can do so more carefully and protect the growing shoots in the centre. Any waste is used to mulch the plants.*

Rɪɢʜᴛ: *Made by the Hopi of Second Mesa in northern Arizona, this deep coiled basket has a foundation of bundles of galleta grass sewn with split yucca leaves. Hopi baskets are often decorated with images of Katchinas, the emissaries of the spirit world.*

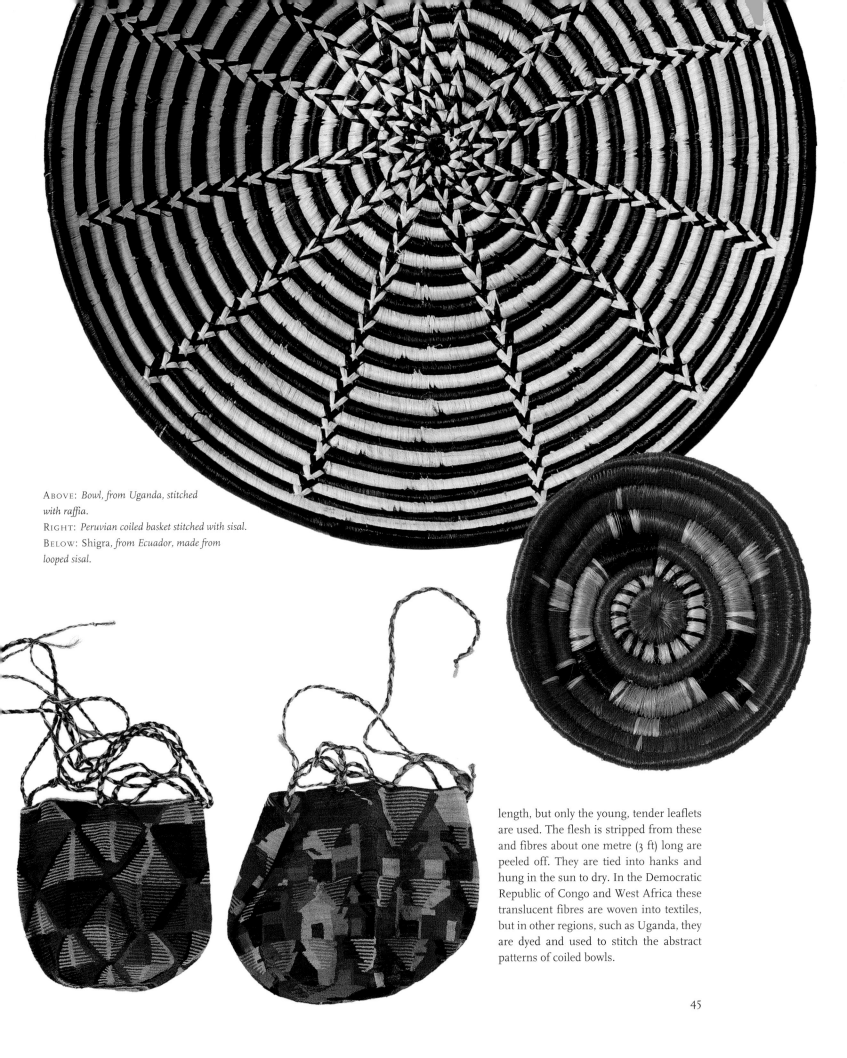

ABOVE: *Bowl, from Uganda, stitched with raffia.*
RIGHT: *Peruvian coiled basket stitched with sisal.*
BELOW: Shigra, *from Ecuador, made from looped sisal.*

length, but only the young, tender leaflets are used. The flesh is stripped from these and fibres about one metre (3 ft) long are peeled off. They are tied into hanks and hung in the sun to dry. In the Democratic Republic of Congo and West Africa these translucent fibres are woven into textiles, but in other regions, such as Uganda, they are dyed and used to stitch the abstract patterns of coiled bowls.

45

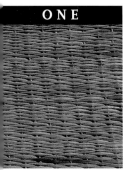

OTHER VEGETAL FIBRES

The world's climate and terrain are so diverse that many regions provide unique habitats where only certain endemic species can survive. The basketmaker has no choice but to be adaptable and use what is available. The range of plants is enormous. If a plant is flexible, long or colourful then the chances are that someone has found a way to exploit it. Apart from the main types of material already discussed in this section, several others are worth mentioning.

Climbing plants

Plants that climb may achieve great lengths and usually vary little in thickness. Once stripped of their rough and often thorny outer layers, plants such as clematis, wisteria, honeysuckle and bramble provide excellent basketmaking materials. They may be used for stake and strand work, in combination with a more rigid material such as willow, or they may be split with a cleave and used for stitching coiled work. English bee hives were generally made of straw coils stitched with bramble.

Vines are widely used in Southeast Asia, the Philippines and Central Africa for plaiting and for stitching coiled baskets. The most sophisticated are the

ABOVE: *A vine rattle from the Democratic Republic of Congo; used by shamen.*
BELOW: *French frame basket with a hazel and willow skeleton, and wild clematis strands.*

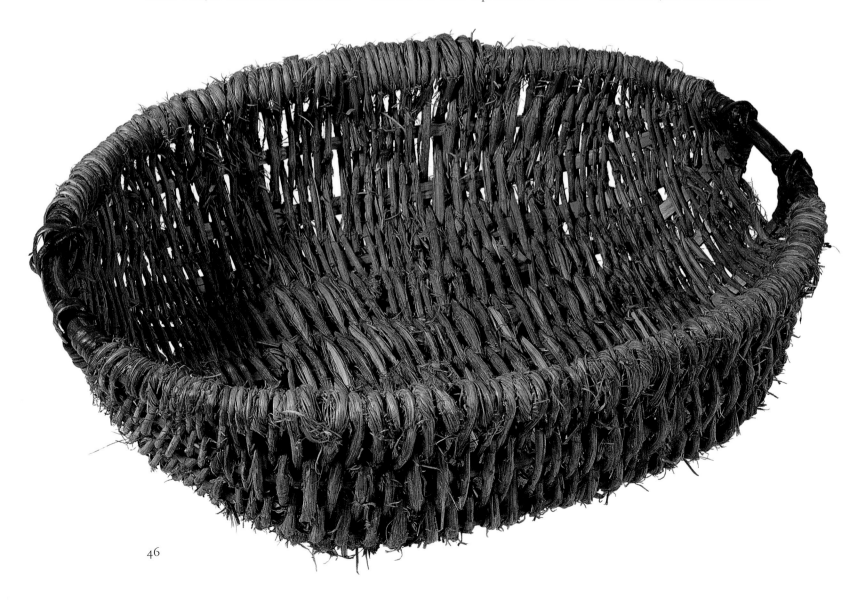

Yan lipao baskets made popular by the Queen of Thailand.

Bast fibres

THE stems of many herbaceous plants such as hemp, milkweed (*Apocynum*) and jute may be soaked, bashed and combed to separate the long, tough fibres. These fibres can be plaited, but are most often used in bundle coiling or stitching.

Bushes and shrubs

THE long whippy stems of many shrubs are often employed in basketmaking. Dogwood, *Cornus* species, is particularly good because of its attractive red or yellow colouring. The Hopi of Third Mesa in Arizona weave their wicker plaques from *Siwi* (*Parryella filifolia*) and *Sivaapi* (rabbitbrush, *Chrysothamnus* spp.), two local, low-growing shrubs with slender stems. These materials, like many others in this period of climatic change, are becoming harder and harder to find and the weavers are turning to alternatives such as rattan imported from Southeast Asia.

Husks and pods

IN North America husks of maize are used to make bags and pouches by the Nez Perce and the Washo of the Great Basin, while in the Southwest stripping the viciously horned seedpods of the devil's claw, *Martynia parviflora*, provides fibres that are employed by many tribes to stitch black patterns on their coiled baskets.

ABOVE, LEFT: *The Hopi of Third Mesa in Arizona weave wicker plaques for ceremonial use from the stems of local shrubs such as rabbitbrush.*
ABOVE, CENTRE: *Behind a Pima olla, or grain basket, stands a large modern Navajo tray with black pattern worked in devil's claw. Today, many Navajos have revived basketmaking skills, incorporating design elements associated with neighbouring tribes such as the Western Apache and the Pima.*
ABOVE, RIGHT: *A Papago 'man in the maze' basket worked in yucca and devil's claw, from southern Arizona.*
RIGHT: *Thai basket of* Yan lipao *vine.*
BELOW: *Baskets, from the Philippines, made using fibre from banana stems.*

SKIN AND HIDE

FOR hunter-gatherer societies and nomadic herdsmen the skins of animals are the most readily available resource. Strips cut from the skins are easy to manipulate, they are tough and, to a great extent, waterproof.

Rawhide

SKINS must be stripped of hair and then dried or salted to prevent them rotting. In this state, the material is known as rawhide. Any work must be carried out while the rawhide is wet and elastic as it becomes stiff and hard as it dries out. Long thin strips called *babiche* are ideal for making snowshoes and are also used to make interlaced chair seating in India and Afghanistan.

Leather

THE life expectancy of hide is prolonged by tanning, a process where the hide is immersed in chemicals, oils or vegetable extracts for some time. Once tanned, the hide is known as leather and will remain soft and flexible. Leather strips are commonly used in North Africa – for warps in the weaving of mats, such as those made by the nomadic Tuareg of the Sahara, or as decorative 'beading' stitched down on coiled baskets.

Reinforcement and fittings

LEATHER strips are frequently used in Europe to make hinges for hampers and straps to fasten them with. Leather has often been employed to protect the vulnerable parts of baskets from wear and tear. The modern Western Apache now use commercially produced suede for this task, whereas the large wicker crates used by the British Post Office to sort the mail once had corners reinforced with whale hide.

Baskets made in many places, for example the *kiondo* baskets of Kenya, are given leather shoulder straps or handles as they are strong, flexible and comfortable.

Decoration

THE most common method of using leather to decorate baskets is in the form of fringes. Examples can be found in the basketry of the Sudan, Namibia and on the Apache burden baskets of the White Mountains in Arizona.

The Fulani of Mali and Niger use leather both to decorate and strengthen their striking, twined grass hats.

ABOVE: *Cree snowshoes from the Canadian Provinces of Saskatchewan or Manitoba. They are strung with* babiche *strips.*

LEFT: *Two reed and leather mats made by the Tuareg, 'the Blue Men of the Sahara'. The Tuareg are a nomadic people with few materials at their disposal apart from what they can obtain from their flocks.*

BELOW: *A coiled grass basket decorated with strips of leather. It was made by the Baggara of North Kordofan in the Sudan.*

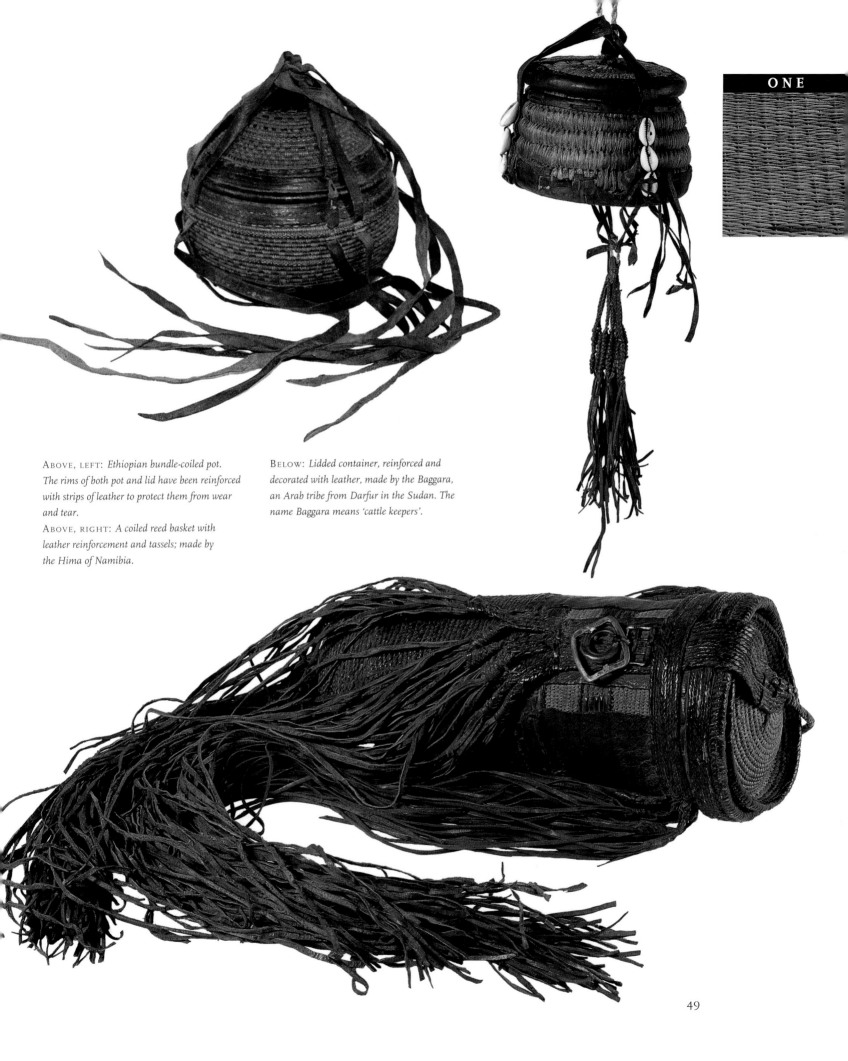

ABOVE, LEFT: *Ethiopian bundle-coiled pot. The rims of both pot and lid have been reinforced with strips of leather to protect them from wear and tear.*

ABOVE, RIGHT: *A coiled reed basket with leather reinforcement and tassels; made by the Hima of Namibia.*

BELOW: *Lidded container, reinforced and decorated with leather, made by the Baggara, an Arab tribe from Darfur in the Sudan. The name Baggara means 'cattle keepers'.*

49

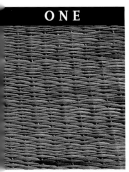

WOOL AND HAIR

Wool

THE wool and hair of sheep, goats, camels, llamas and even dogs can be processed into yarn. Both must be brushed or carded until all the fibres lie in one direction and then spun, either by hand or wheel, into a strong, twisted strand of indefinite length. They are flexible, have an attractive sheen and are easy to dye.

Uses and distribution

NOMADS and herdsmen around the world have taken advantage of wool as an excellent medium for making baskets. Coiled grass baskets with wool stitching are made by many groups better known for their prowess at rug weaving. These include the Qashq'ai of Iran, the Berber of the Moroccan Atlas Mountains and the Navajo of the Four Corners country in the USA.

BELOW, LEFT: *Navajo wedding basket with wool stitching by Eliela Bellie of Winslow, Arizona.*
BELOW, RIGHT: *Papago horsehair miniature which is only 6 cm (2¹/₈ in.) in diameter.*

Wool has also been used – in the form of tufts and tassels – to decorate baskets, for instance, unexpectedly, on the coiled straw baskets of the Alaskan Eskimos.

Horsehair

LONG, tough hairs plucked from the manes and tails of horses are occasionally used in basketmaking. They cannot be spun because they are too stiff, but they are available in a range of natural tones, including black, white and a wide selection of browns. On occasion, imitation horsehair baskets have been made from nylon fishing line.

Uses and distribution

ALTHOUGH horsehair is sometimes used for both the bundles and stitching of full-scale baskets, it is far more suited to the manufacture of miniature basketry. Tiny versions of traditional baskets are now made commercially by women of the Papago (Tohono O'odham), who live south of Phoenix in Arizona, USA. In Rari, Chile, miniature baskets are made, as well as small figures and trinkets, using dyed horsehair wrapped around a core of plant fibre.

ABOVE: *Bridles and quirts were often made from horsehair by tribes from the American Plateau and Basin regions such as the Utes and Shoshone. Dyed horsehair is coiled around a rawhide core and fixed using a method resembling the soumak textile technique. Horse trappings were frequently made by prisoners serving time in the state penitentiaries.*
OPPOSITE, BELOW: *Two coiled pots, stitched with wool, used by Berber women from the Midelt district of the Middle Atlas Mountains in Morocco to hold personal items.*

Human hair

IN a society such as that of the Iban in Sarawak, where head hunting was once a common practice, human hair was woven into special offering baskets made for feasts in memory of a family's heroic ancestors.

Locks of hair from a departed loved one were treasured in nineteenth-century England by the Victorians and were often woven into elaborate braids and chains.

ABOVE, LEFT: *Miniature set of nesting baskets made from horsehair in Chile.*
ABOVE, RIGHT: *A coiled pot stitched with wool by a Qashq'ai nomad from southwest Iran.*

51

METAL

BASKETMAKING techniques have been used to make objects from metal strips and wire since ancient times. Among the artefacts excavated at Etruscan sites in Italy (pre 400 BC) was a bronze bed sprung with interlaced metal strips. Metal is tough and lasts a very long time, which makes it ideal for bearing heavy loads, but it can also be drawn out into very fine wire suitable for making miniatures and fine art objects.

Techniques

WIRE is long, thin and round in section, like most basketmaking materials, so it can be employed when using many regular basketry methods, although bending and twisting it can be hard work. Interlacing is a simple method, but interlinking in a 'corn dolly' weave is frequently used as wire, once bent, will hold its shape.

Uses

STAINLESS steel and brass are often used to make kitchenware since they are rustproof and heatproof and ideal for rigid openwork structures. Wire strainers for frying in oil are widespread in both East and West, while salad spinners and egg baskets are common in Europe.

Wire birdcages often resemble bamboo structures, but may exploit the qualities of wire to form convoluted and elaborate shapes. On the other hand, chicken-wire and chainlink fences are simply constructed, but make extremely effective large-scale barriers.

Many masterpieces of antique silver-ware imitating the form and structure of baskets were once made in Europe, although they were often pierced and cast rather than interlaced. These elaborate items were frequently used as table ornaments by the well-to-do.

ABOVE: *An Ethiopian milk bottle waterproofed with acacia gum and decorated with metal strips.*
BELOW: *Wire baskets from Scandinavia (left), and from Arizona, made by Wayne Pedro of Pan Tak (right); miniatures from China (front left and centre) and Thailand (front right).*

ABOVE: *Ladles for deep frying, Thailand.*
RIGHT: *French wire egg basket.*
BELOW: *Zulu telephone-wire basket (*imbenge*)*.

Many modern baskets, mass produced in the East for the fashionable European interior design market, are now made on a rigid wire frame interlaced with natural fibres such as rattan or seagrass.

Telephone wire

ZULUS from southern Africa traditionally use inverted coiled baskets called *imbenge* to cover their clay beer pots. Migrant workers in the cities in the 1980s adapted their skills to make *imbenge* from local materials – plastic-covered telephone wire. The wire *imbenge* is worked over an enamel dish, which acts as a mould, and has a linked structure as coiling is harder to work with wire. These colourful baskets are now becoming rarer as many makers have damaged their hands on the unforgiving wire and fibre optics have superseded wire in telecommunications.

SYNTHETIC FIBRES

Dᴜʀɪɴɢ the twentieth century items made from plastics and synthetic fibres usurped the place of traditional basketry in many parts of the world. Factory-made shopping bags, laundry baskets, sieves, buckets and nets are now universally available, often at a much lower price than items made locally from natural materials. Binder twine, polypropylene straps and synthetic sacking, the waste products of modern packaging, have all been recycled to make baskets and on occasion such materials have even been purchased new, specially for basketmaking.

Necessity

Tʜᴇ lack of traditional materials due to industrialization, modern agricultural methods and environmental changes has led enterprising craftworkers to take advantage of the flexible and virtually indestructible properties of synthetic strips and incorporate them into their baskets. In Mali, for instance, coiled baskets used for storing dry foodstuffs were once made from grasses and bark and stitched with strips of bark, but, as it has become very difficult to acquire suitable bark, they are now stitched with strips cut from old nylon rice sacks. In Gambia grass baskets are stitched with narrow strips of binder tape salvaged from packaged goods.

Decoration

Pʟᴀsᴛɪᴄs come in a wide range of colours. In Europe and the USA, during the first part of the twentieth century, designers were excited by the new synthetic fibres and their decorative possibilities. Basketmakers, such as those making Southport boat baskets in England, incorporated strips of plastic into their baskets because of their colour and resilience. Now Westerners tend to look upon plastic as being cheap and nasty, but in the developing world the possibilities are still being explored. In Nubia it is not unusual to find a basket made from coiled plastic washing line, while in Mexico plastic is not out of place among the bright coloured materials that craftsmen prefer.

Imitation

Aʟᴛʜᴏᴜɢʜ plastic and nylon can be moulded into any shape, it is ironic that an allusion is often made to original basket structures. Many modern laundry baskets, for instance, are moulded in such a way that they appear to have an inter-laced structure, toy prams resemble wicker cradles and planters are made to look like flower baskets, complete with braided handles. Even in this age of technology, the appeal of natural fibres and hand craftsmanship is still recognized and emulated.

Tᴏᴘ: *Plastic baskets at Alanya market, Turkey.*
Aʙᴏᴠᴇ: *Fashionable synthetic basket, 1998.*
Oᴘᴘᴏsɪᴛᴇ, ᴀʙᴏᴠᴇ, ʟᴇꜰᴛ: *Twill-plaited basket from Mexico. This is an example of traditional Mexican basketry, apart from the use of synthetic rather than natural materials.*
Oᴘᴘᴏsɪᴛᴇ, ᴀʙᴏᴠᴇ, ʀɪɢʜᴛ: *A tray from Taiwan with gaudy plastic beads strung on monofilament thread.*
Oᴘᴘᴏsɪᴛᴇ, ʙᴇʟᴏᴡ: *Brightly coloured basket made from packing tape by Lois Walpole, a British basketmaker, who specializes in the use of homegrown and recycled materials.*

Lᴇꜰᴛ: *Centre cane basket, with plastic detailing, made in England in the 1950s or 1960s.*
Rɪɢʜᴛ: *Plastic imitates bamboo here, a Hmong hill-tribe basket from northern Thailand.*

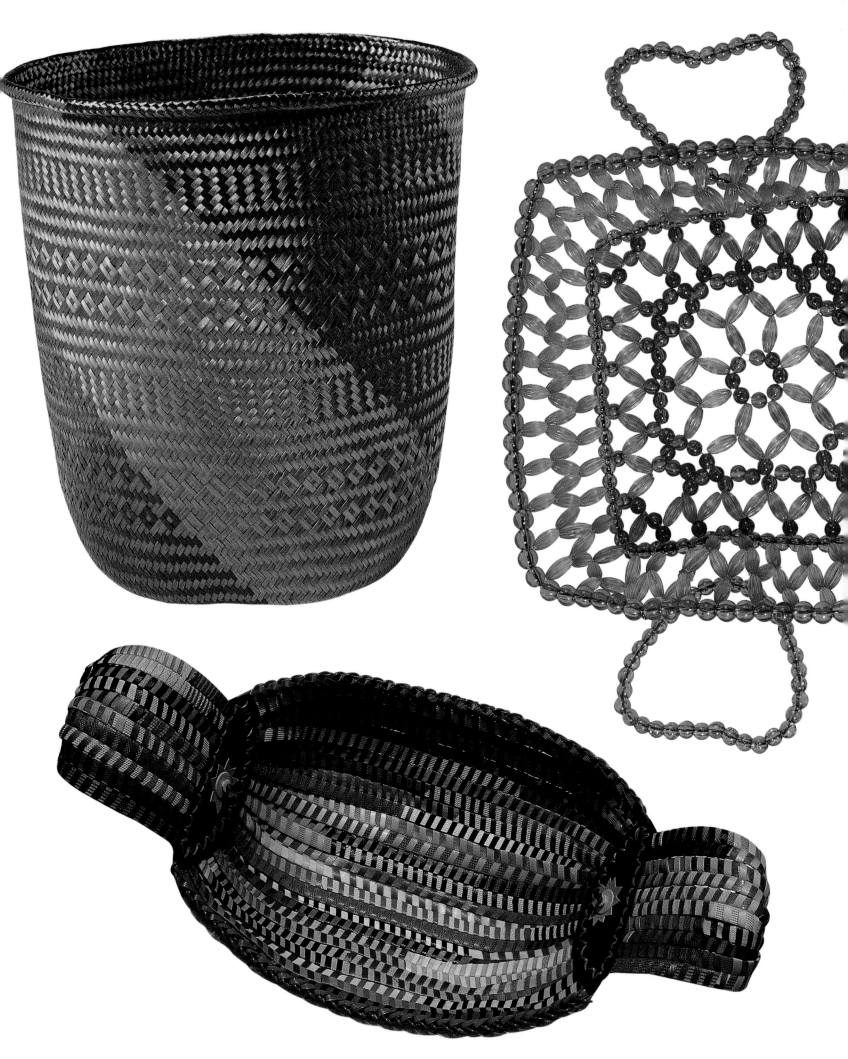

FAR LEFT: *Baskets from around the world.*
LEFT: Imbenges *from South Africa; made using two different techniques.*

TECHNIQUES

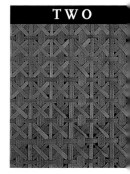

TWO

LEFT: *Coiled plait food cover from Zanzibar.*
BELOW, LEFT: *Painted Chinese food basket.*
BELOW, RIGHT: *Barotse rod-coiled basket from Zambia.*

TECHNIQUES

D IFFERENT basketry techniques evolve all over the world – every basketmaker has his or her own way of doing things, each fibre manipulated has its own character and each problem faced has a different solution. However, in any one area craftsmen face the same problems and traditional methods are established. Within these limitations the true artist is able to improvise.

MATERIALS AND TECHNIQUES

T HE properties of the materials used to make baskets vary enormously – some are stiff, some flexible, some are long, some short. Accordingly, the techniques required to turn them into baskets are diverse. Broad, flat materials can be plaited, flimsy fibres can be bundled together, and long pliant fibres can be twined or interlaced.

ABOVE, LEFT: *Owen Jones making a Cumberland swill, an English frame basket, fashioned from riven oak.*
ABOVE, RIGHT: *Making a stake and strand storage basket in Mandu, Madhya Pradesh, India.*
LEFT: *A young girl in Zanzibar plaiting a basket from strips of pandanus.*
RIGHT: *A Polish basketmaker weaving a square stake and strand basket from willow.*
OPPOSITE, ABOVE, LEFT: *Harvesting mulberry leaves in openwork baskets to feed silkworms, Murcia, Spain.*

OPPOSITE, ABOVE, RIGHT: *Rattan stake and strand baskets used by Yarmouth cod fishermen from Suffolk, England. The open sides are held together with fitching.*

OPPOSITE, BELOW, LEFT: *Hopi basketmaker from Oraibi, Third Mesa, Arizona, making a wicker plaque. On Second Mesa basketmakers specialize in coiled basketry.*

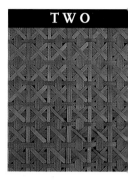

FUNCTION AND TECHNIQUES

T HE range of items – round, rectangular, flat or cylindrical – that can be constructed using basketmaking techniques is considerable. Their shape depends on their intended function. A basket or tray for winnowing or drying food must be shallow, but a storage jar needs to be tall and capacious. A sleeping mat must be flat and densely woven, but a fish trap needs to be rigid and have an openwork structure. In any traditional community several techniques are normally to be found, each employed in making baskets with a particular function. On Second Mesa in Arizona, for instance, Hopi ceremonial plaques are made from coils of galleta grass finely stitched with yucca fibre, baskets for sifting corn are made from plaited yucca, while burden baskets and cradles are made from the stems of local shrubs using the stake and strand method.

GLOBAL DIVERSITY

I T IS interesting to observe that distinctive forms of basketry have developed in far flung places because of the local materials available and the lifestyle. However, perhaps because of the restrictions of the materials or cultural similarities, there may also be at times a startling similarity between items produced by societies thousands of miles apart.

LEFT: *Judy Simpson making a willow stake and strand basket, Cambridgeshire, England.*
ABOVE, LEFT: *Plaiting hats in Madagascar.*
ABOVE, RIGHT: *Harvesting oysters in a frame basket, Arcachon, France.*

COILING

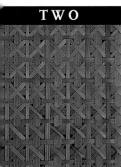

THE remains of coiled baskets have been excavated in some of the world's most ancient settlements. At Fayum, an early Egyptian site in the Libyan desert southwest of Cairo, fragments were found that have been dated back to 5200 BC, although they may date back even further. Baskets of coiled straw were among the treasures discovered in southern Turkey at Çatal Hüyük, one of the world's first towns, already established in *c.* 6250 BC. It has even been suggested that the technique of coiled pottery was copied from ancient basketry.

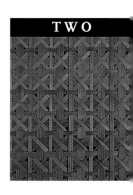

OPPOSITE, ABOVE: *Rod-coiled basket made by the Barotse/Lozi of Zambia. Ifugao baskets from the Philippines often closely resemble Barotse basketry.*

OPPOSITE, CENTRE: *Small, rock-solid coiled Barotse pot (5.5 cm, 2 in. high).*

OPPOSITE, INSET: *Datsolalee, the famous Washo basketmaker, surrounded by examples of her work.*

LEFT: *Modern Navajo basket, by Wayne Holiday, with a coil foundation of stacked rods. Since the 1970s the enterprising Navajo of the American Southwest have revitalized basketmaking using innovative designs which incorporate elements of the styles of neighbouring tribes.*

BELOW: *Rod coiled basket, from Vietnam, made from rattan.*

BOTTOM: *Latvian basket made from coiled pine root stitched with willow.*

Materials

To make a coiled basket the raw materials must either come in long lengths or it has to be easy to join them into an indefinite length. Creepers such as rattan, which can grow as long as 135 metres (450 ft), are perfect for coiling, but short, delicate grasses also serve the purpose well when twisted into a bundle or plaited together. The fragility of the materials often belies the strength of the basket. Rods will obviously ensure a tougher, more rigid basket than bundles of soft fibres.

The material used to stitch the coils together must be tough, but flexible, and again length is an advantage. Split spruce roots, yucca fibre, brambles, reeds and cotton have all been used and in recent years tough modern materials such as polypropylene strapping and strips of recycled synthetic sacking have been utilized in places where traditional materials have become hard to come by.

APACHE THREE-ROD COILING

Rod coiling

ROD COILING is a process where the coils are made from either a single rod or up to five stacked or bunched rods.

Most coiled baskets are made by starting with a flat spiral which begins at the centre of the base. Each turn is secured by binding or stitching it to the previous one, although a tough material like rattan may sometimes even be nailed in place with bamboo splints, as in the case of the *sika* or hanging baskets from Bangladesh. Stitches may or may not interlock with previous rows.

Successive coils are added, overlapping the previous ones to create curved or vertical sides. In this way bowl, cylinder, cone and jar shapes are all easy to construct.

Baskets of coiled rods are made, using a variety of materials, in places as widespread as New Mexico and Myanmar (Burma). The Barotse of Zambia make baskets that are so solid that they cannot be compressed, even when applying pressure with both hands. Some of the baskets made by Datsolalee, the Washo basketmaker from Nevada, employed as many as thirty stitches to the inch, 50,000 in total for a basket!

BUNDLE COILING

I<small>N</small> the absence of raw materials of any length, basketmakers have frequently resorted to gathering flexible, short fibres, such as grasses, reeds or straw, into bundles that can be bound together and extended by constantly adding and binding more material.

TWO

Technique

A<small>SPIRALLING</small> coil of bundles is built up in the same way as rods (see pp. 60–61), although the starting-point is sometimes a square-shaped knot. However, as work proceeds new material must constantly be added to extend the bundle. In Britain new straw is added by feeding it through a collar of cow's horn to maintain an even thickness.

A<small>BOVE</small>, <small>RIGHT</small>: *Coiling palm bundles in Nigeria.*
B<small>ELOW</small>: *Lidded grain basket of coiled grass from Lesotho. Similar baskets are also made by the Zulu, who call them* iqutho.

Stitching

T<small>RADITIONALLY</small>, whether in Britain, Africa or the USA, coils are sewn together with the aid of a bone awl to pierce the bundles. Flexible fibres, like those obtained from palms or yuccas, are required for stitching, although thicker materials, such as willow, brambles or roots, may be split into suitably flexible strips. The style of stitching and the colour of the materials used can be exploited to create complex and striking patterns.

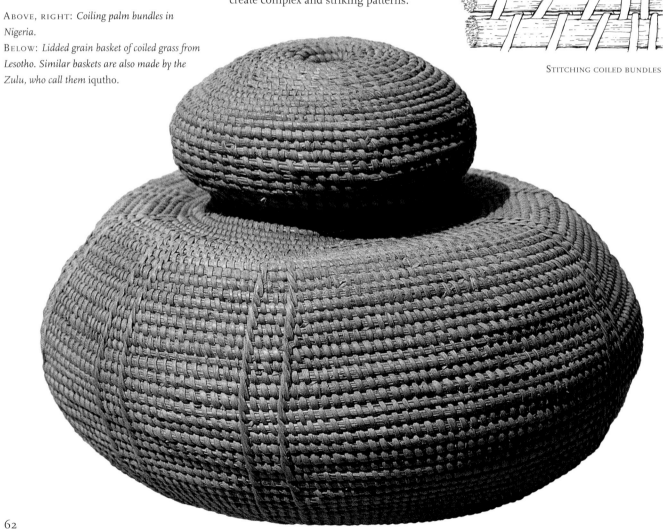

S<small>TITCHING COILED BUNDLES</small>

Distribution

THE technique of constructing baskets by stitching coiled bundles of soft vegetable fibres is very widespread. It is particularly common on prairies and savannahs throughout the world, in marshy regions and also where the cultivation of grain produces straw as a waste product.

In Britain and western Europe rye straw 'lipwork' is used to construct many items such as the traditional bee skep and in the windy Orkney Islands, north of mainland Scotland, chairs are made with a distinctive oatstraw back and hood.

Some basketmakers have exploited the softness and flexibility of grass to make smooth, delicate baskets, like those made by the Tutsi of Rwanda and Burundi, while others, such as the Pima Indians of Arizona, have seen the ready availability of the raw materials as an opportunity to build storage vessels of prodigious size.

BELOW: *A Papago bowl, from south of Phoenix, Arizona, constructed with a foundation of bear grass stitched with yucca.*

TOP: *East African coiled basket; in places the palm stitching has been worn away, revealing the foundation of bundled grass.*

ABOVE, LEFT: *Two containers, from Ethiopia, constructed with a foundation of thick bundles typical of the region.*

ABOVE, RIGHT: *A Mapuche woman from southern Chile making coiled baskets with widely spaced stitching.*

LEFT: *Group of Tutsi igiseke from Rwanda or Uganda. These beautiful baskets are constructed over a wooden mould using very fine bundles of silky grasses.*

PLAIT COILING

FIBRES can be extended, so that they can be coiled, by plaiting them into a braid. Braids have more structural integrity than loose bundles and can be bent at angles acute enough to make square basketry possible. A plaited braid will lie flat and butt up or overlap neatly when being coiled. A plait also has a distinctive, attractive pattern created by the texture of interweaving strands. Baskets of this type have been in existence for 5,000 years, if not longer.

Technique

THE simplest plait used for coiled basketry is braided with the same technique that people all over the world use to braid their hair – three strands laid longitudinally side by side. Employing a greater number of strands produces a wider braid more suited to coiling. As the braid is coiled it can be attached to the previous turn in several ways. If the braid is completed before coiling commences, the turns can simply be sewn together with thread or twine. If plaiting is carried out at the same time as the coiling, the link can be made by leaving strands sticking out from the sides of the braid which can be woven into the following turn. A virtually invisible link can also be achieved by incorporating a cord into one edge of the braid around which the subsequent turn can be worked.

OPPOSITE, ABOVE: *Coiled plait mat from Zanzibar. The braids are anchored by a hidden cord as plaiting proceeds.*
OPPOSITE, BELOW: *An esparto grass basket made from stitched fifteen-strand braid and used for carrying loads. Similar baskets can be found all along the shores of the Mediterranean.*
INSET: *Weighing coiled plait baskets containing sulphur on the quayside at Catania, Sicily, in the early twentieth century.*

It is usually possible to identify a coiled plait basket from its spiralling base, the ridges on the inside where the coils have been stitched and the uneven rim where the final coil ends.

Distribution and uses

THE most common use for plait coiling is in the making of mats or hats. In Europe and the USA coiled wheat straw plaits are the chosen material for straw hats for gondoliers, school children, butchers, and women attending formal functions. In nineteenth-century Cambridgeshire bonnets were also made by professional milliners using crested dog's tail grass, *Cynosurus cristatus*, a softer material that allowed for the better bending and shaping of curved surfaces.

ST PAUL FLEEING DAMASCUS, AFTER A MOSAIC IN THE MEDIEVAL ROYAL PALACE IN PALERMO, SICILY

In parts of Asia and around the Mediterranean strong baskets made from plaits have been used for shifting loads since ancient times. An interesting reference is to be found in the Bible in 2 Corinthians 11, xxxiii, in which St Paul describes how he was lowered in a basket over the walls of Damascus to escape the angry mob. He uses the Greek word *sargane* which means specifically a basket of plaited cords.

TOP: *Zulu mat made from coiled grass plaits, South Africa.*
ABOVE: *A common type of Indian labourer's basket of coiled palm fibre with a hidden foundation cord.*
LEFT: *Two 'shopping' baskets. The larger is from Essaouira, Morocco, and the smaller is a souvenir from the Algarve, Portugal.*
BELOW: *Collecting ground meal in a coiled basket in the Algarve, Portugal.*

PLAITING

PLAITING, or oblique interlacing, is employed in the construction of fabric far wider than braids. It is the simplest method of interweaving two elements of equal thickness and flexibility, and is widely used in the manufacture of articles that require a flat, even surface. Although sometimes worked on horizontal and vertical axes, the most sophisticated plaited basketry is worked on the diagonal. Plaited basketry requires wide, flat strips which can be made from materials such as split bamboo, reeds or palm fronds.

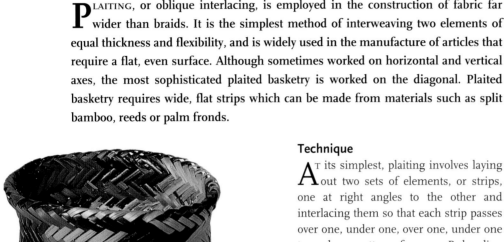

Technique

AT its simplest, plaiting involves laying out two sets of elements, or strips, one at right angles to the other and interlacing them so that each strip passes over one, under one, over one, under one to produce a pattern of squares. By bending the work in progress vertically, adjacent surfaces can be interlaced to form three-dimensional shapes such as bags and boxes.

LEFT: 1/1 PLAIN WEAVE

Colour placement

AN experienced plaiter knows that by laying out each set of elements with a careful sequence of colours, a pattern will be revealed as the two sets are woven together. The simplest patterns are stripes and checks, but elaborate grids, zigzags, stripes and dots are all possible without any further manipulation.

Twilling

THE use of twilling, in which one strand passes over two or more others, creates a stronger and more impervious surface. It also makes it possible to create an even greater diversity of pattern, both abstract and figurative.

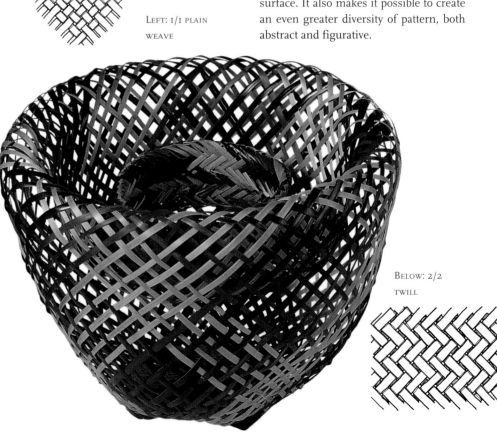

BELOW: 2/2 TWILL

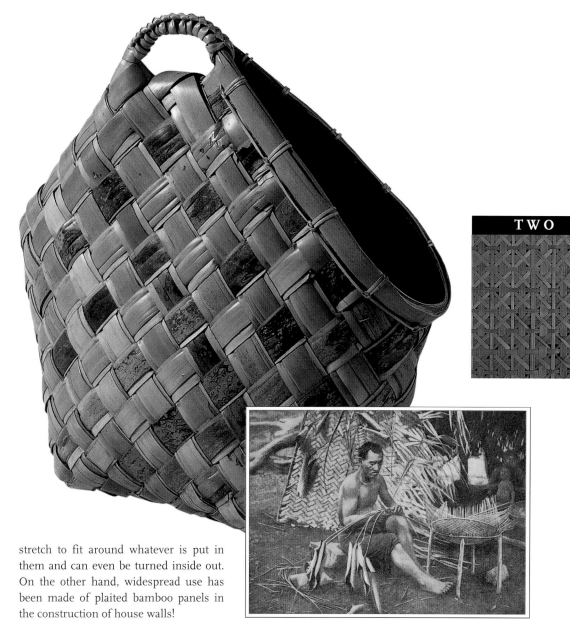

OPPOSITE, ABOVE: *Maori* kete, *from New Zealand, plaited using* Phormium tenax. *The texture of the plain weave has been varied in the top section by splitting each strand in two.*

OPPOSITE, BELOW: *A pair of flexible* cundu *baskets twill plaited from* chocolatillo *fibre in Colombia by Waunana people.*

RIGHT: *A* takul, *from Karangasem in Bali, for carrying a cockerel; plaited in plain weave from strips of palm leaf.*

INSET: *Waiomgomo Indian, from Venezuela, plaiting a large sieve. A twill-plaited panel is leaning up behind him.*

BELOW: *A hat and gift basket from Gianyar in northern Bali. The patterns have been created using the colour placement method.*

Uses and distribution

PLAITING is, in essence, such a simple technique that variations have been developed all around the world. Finely plaited baskets are made from split bamboo, rattan or grasses in many places and used for a wide range of daily tasks. Openweave *cundu* baskets plaited on the coast of Colombia are so flexible that they stretch to fit around whatever is put in them and can even be turned inside out. On the other hand, widespread use has been made of plaited bamboo panels in the construction of house walls!

MULTI-DIRECTIONAL PLAITING

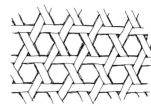

PLAITING is conventionally constructed on two axes, but it is also possible to operate using three or more axes in a process known as multi-axial or multi-directional plaiting or interlacing. When worked tightly on three axes, a distinctive pattern of hexagons or triangles is produced. Popularly referred to as hex weave, it is a technique frequently used to make openwork baskets which are both strong and light.

Openwork baskets

AN openwork framework is ideal for many purposes as it is light and requires less material than other techniques and is therefore both cheaper and less time consuming to make. By employing a structure based on a horizontal and two diagonals, the maximum strength can be achieved with a minimum of materials.

ABOVE, RIGHT: *Man making a strong, but light, hex-weave back pack in the mountains of Nepal. Back packs are particularly common in hilly regions.*

BELOW: *A large hat from southern China. It is constructed from two layers of split bamboo, woven in hex weave, with a layer of banana leaves sandwiched between them.*

PLAITING ON THREE AXES

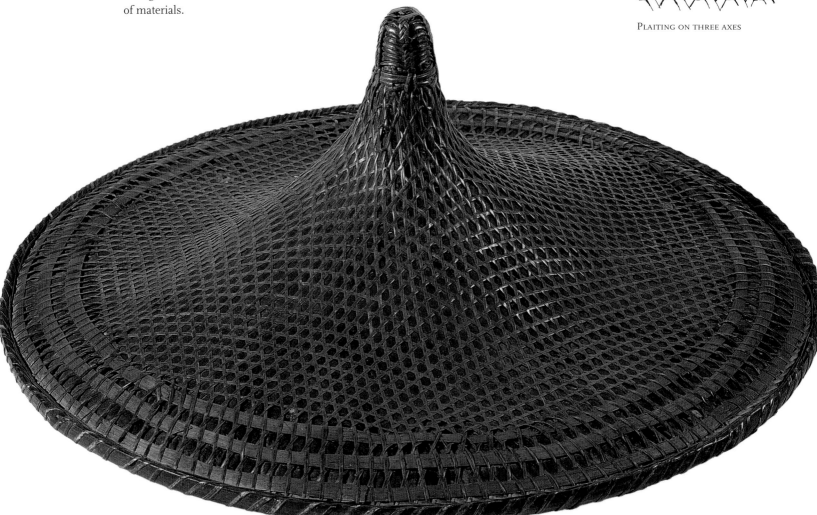

RIGHT: *A double-walled split bamboo basket from Kiryu, sixty miles north of the Japanese capital, Tokyo. Reinforcing a stake and strand basket with a hex-weave shell has made this basket very strong.*

Open basketwork constructed on three axes is particularly common in Asia where it is used in many ways – for strong but light burden baskets, for livestock containers and for the interior structure of hats.

Tightly woven baskets

WHEN the interweaving of the separate elements is pulled tightly together a tough, rigid structure is formed as it is, in effect, several layers thick. Most often this technique is used on a fairly small scale in the making of pots and boxes. Decoration can be added with elements of contrasting colours. Dynamic patterns, incorporating triangles, hexagons, stars and diamonds, can be created.

BELOW, LEFT: *Pandanus box from Palawan Island in the Philippines. In Southeast Asia tightly woven hex weave is known as 'broken rice' or 'mad weave'.*
BELOW, RIGHT: *A split-cane chair back woven by Kay Johnson, England.*

Chair caning

THE most familiar form of this technique in the West is the caning of chairs with split rattan, a process introduced to England during the reign of Charles II in the seventeenth century. It had been developed in northeast India to make comfortable seats for rattan chairs and was subsequently employed by English craftsmen to make seats for elegant walnut and cheaper beechwood chairs. There are many variations, some worked in three directions, others in four. The frame of the chair is drilled so the cane can be threaded through to secure it and stretch it across the frame. Work is carried out on one axis at a time and becomes more difficult with each successive diagonal as it must be laced in and out of all those preceding it.

TWINING

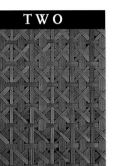

TWINING is a system of basketmaking that is most often used to construct items that have a degree of flexibility, but will hold their shape. The materials used are fine, pliant ones such as grasses or leaf fibres.

Technique

TWO sets of elements are required, one passive and one active. Normally both are of the same material. The passive elements, or warps, are laid out either vertically or radiating from the centre. The active elements, or wefts, are worked in pairs in and out of the warps. One passes over the passive warp and the other passes under and then they are twisted so that they swap over, the first passing under and the other over the warp. This process is repeated, twisting the pair in the same direction between each warp.

TWINING IN TWO COLOURS

Twining produces a dense weave, slightly ribbed and with a distinctive diagonal twist to the wefts. The warps are normally completely concealed.

Pattern making

THE texture of a simply twined basket is attractive in its own right, but a pattern can be introduced in two ways for a more dramatic impact. A subtle pattern can be woven by twilling or by changing the direction in which the wefts are twisted, according to a planned sequence. This type of pattern, like damask cloth, is only revealed by the play of light on the surface. A superb example of this method is the

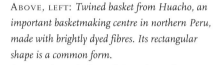

ABOVE, LEFT: *Twined basket from Huacho, an important basketmaking centre in northern Peru, made with brightly dyed fibres. Its rectangular shape is a common form.*
ABOVE: *A pouch, from Gujarat in northwest India, made of densely twined goat hair.*
BELOW, LEFT: *Two baskets used to carry market produce, for storage or for collecting locusts. They are made from twined, natural and brightly dyed savannah grass in the Bolgatang district of northern Ghana.*
BELOW: *Twining the base of a savannah grass basket in Accra, Ghana.*

delicately patterned hats made by the Fulani of Mali.

The second method requires that the two wefts of the twining pair are not of the same colour. This means that with every twist a different colour will be brought to the surface. A classic example is the colourful patterning of savannah grass baskets made in Ghana.

A whole range of complicated decorative techniques exists which can be used to created sophisticated figurative designs.

These are discussed in section three which covers all aspects of decoration.

Uses and distribution

TWINING is used to make tough, hardwearing items such as bags and hats. Examples can be found on every inhabited continent, but the finest examples are probably those made by the peoples of subsaharan and Central Africa, and the Native American peoples of the western United States and Canada.

TOP: *Three twined baskets from Zimbabwe. The warps are of twigs or split cane twined with ilala palm. Similar buskets are also made using the stake and strand technique.*

ABOVE, LEFT: *Three Chinese twined rush baskets made for export. The one on the right was bought in Rhodesia (now Zimbabwe) in the 1960s.*

ABOVE, RIGHT: *Twined grass basket for carrying produce; bought in Tanzania.*

STAKE AND STRAND 1

T<small>HIS</small> method of construction, like plaiting, uses two sets of interlaced elements. However one set, known as the stakes, is rigid and passive, while the other more flexible set, known as strands or weavers, is manipulated in and out of the stakes.

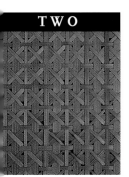

TWO

Materials

B<small>ECAUSE</small> of their flexibility, coppiced woods such as willow are ideal for this technique and frequently the method is referred to as 'wicker' (from the Scandinavian *vika*, meaning to bend). In many regions of the world considerable expertise has been acquired by exponents of this technique using other materials such as bamboo and rattan in the East and cleft wood splints in Europe and North America.

Technique

W<small>ORK</small> begins with the base. A cross or 'slath' is formed from two sets of rods at right angles to each other. One set may be slit so the others can be slotted through them. Weavers are then introduced and wound around to bind the slath together. As work progresses, the rods are splayed out and interwoven so that eventually a round structure of the desired size is achieved. This is then trimmed.

A<small>BOVE</small>: *A French stake and strand basket made by Emilien Metezeau using white willow weavers and split ash for the stakes. The rim is an unpeeled willow rod.*

B<small>ELOW, LEFT</small>: *Hopi wicker plaque from Hotevilla, Third Mesa, Arizona. Although many plaques are sold to visitors, they remain an important part of Hopi culture and religion.*

B<small>ELOW</small>: *The base of a Chinese bamboo pot, showing the 'chrysanthemum' beginning.*

B<small>OTTOM</small>: *The base of an English oval market basket made by Jonathan Gordon from brown and white willow.*

O<small>PPOSITE, MIDDLE</small>: *Skeined willow cat basket.*

O<small>PPOSITE, BOTTOM LEFT</small>: *Willow shopping basket with French randing.*

O<small>PPOSITE, BELOW, RIGHT</small>: *Wicker hat from Bahia, Brazil.*

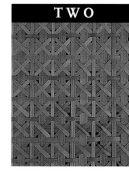

ABOVE, LEFT: *Greek* Arundo donax *basket with English randing.*
ABOVE, MIDDLE: *English willow fruit-picking basket; English randing.*
ABOVE, RIGHT: *Willow basket from Guernsey; French randing.*

To create the walls of the basket new rods are inserted into the base and then bent upwards to serve as stakes, a procedure known as 'upsetting'. They are held in place by weaving strands in and out of them from the bottom to the top of the basket.

In the East the stakes are initially arranged like a star or chrysanthemum and reach to the top of the finished basket.

Randing

RANDING is the simplest type of interweaving, taking one weaver at a time and lacing it in and out of an odd number of vertical stakes, round and round the basket, until it has all been used.

At this point a new rod is inserted, butt first, and work continues in the same way, adding new rods as required. This is known as 'English' randing and can be recognized easily as it creates a regular pattern of even ribs.

'French' randing differs in that a number of weavers are started at the same time, one at each stake. As each weaver is woven in above the one on the next stake this creates a diagonal pattern that winds up the basket. The weavers taper at the same time and produce a denser band towards the top. The point at which a new set of weavers begins can be spotted by the change in density.

TWO

Variations on randing

Randing is the most common technique in stake and strand basketry. For more elaborate textured effects such as herringbone, chevron or diagonal patterns, a 'twill' or 'Japanese weave' technique can be employed, passing weavers over or under more than one stake at a time.

'Slewing' creates a solid effect – in which two or more weavers are woven in together – that can be executed with great speed. It is also called 'double weave'.

Pairing

Pairing is exactly the same as twining. Working from left to right, the normal direction of work, a pair of strands are worked in tandem, one starting in front and one behind. Between each stake the pair are twisted clockwise, the strand behind passing above the other to the front. Strands woven in this way can be tightly packed together with few gaps.

Fitching

Fitching is essentially the reverse of pairing, the pair of strands are twisted anti-clockwise between each stake. In England fitching is frequently employed in openwork basketry as the twisting together of the weavers creates a greater structural integrity than randing with the same number of rods. You can often spot it on wastepaper baskets, cheese platters, lobster pots or runner bean 'wigwams'. It is, however, a technique seldom used in other parts of Europe.

Waling

The top and bottom of the walls of a stake and strand basket are frequently reinforced with strong, densely woven bands called wales. Waling has a very solid look as most of each strand appears at the front of the work.

A wale at the bottom secures the stakes in the base and sets the form of the basket, hence the term 'upsett'. Three or four rods

ABOVE: *Selling flowers on the streets of London in the early twentieth century. The walls of the basket are slewed.*
BELOW, LEFT: *Wheeled shopping basket with brown willow slewing and buff waling.*
BELOW, RIGHT: *Basket, from the Czech Republic, with bands of brown willow waling. The French randing is slewed in the top section.*

RIGHT: THREE-STRAND
WALING

ABOVE: *Large rattan basket formerly used at a textile mill in Colchester, England (45 cm, 17½ in. high). The base, top and centre (to which a handle is attached) are reinforced with bands of waling.*
RIGHT: *A willow basket made by Kay Johnson in the style of a German bride's basket. They would have been commissioned by the bride's godmother. The patterns were often painted, but here they are created by French randing over two, under two and alternating the colours of the weavers.*

are worked at a time, with their ends pushed into the base to the right of the upsett stakes. Each rod then crosses in front of two or more stakes and then behind one, working right round the basket four or more times.

The top wale is worked in much the same way, adding strength and rigidity to the top of the basket before the working of a final border. A number of different techniques are used to make a rim or border. Usually the stakes are bent over and interlaced before being pushed back down into the weave of the basket or cut off short.

75

FRAME BASKETS

Frame, or ribbed, baskets are generally made using the stake and strand method, except that initially a frame is formed from a hoop or hoops of a more rigid material that will define the shape of the completed basket. The 'ose', or hen basket, is a form believed to have been invented in Scotland during Celtic times, but similar forms have been created all around the world.

The one-hoop frame

A stick of willow, hazel or chestnut, about the thickness of a thumb, is thoroughly soaked and bent into a circle or ellipse using the thigh for leverage. The two ends, which have been slyped (cut to a taper) so they will fit neatly, are then nailed or bound together.

Passive stakes or ribs are attached from end to end and weaving begins – a strand is worked back and forth, wrapping around the hoop at each side. Work may progress from either one end or the other, but more often from both ends towards the middle to ensure even tension.

The two-hoop frame

When two hoops are used they are usually attached at right angles so that one defines the rim of the basket and the other the handle and bottom. In the Americas an elaborate lashing, known as 'ojo de dios' or 'God's eye', taking its name from a symbol used by the Huichol of northwest Mexico, is employed.

Above: *Skeined willow basket with two hazel hoops; probably Italian.*
Left: *A cyntell, a Welsh willow frame basket used to collect potatoes; made by D. J. Davies.*
Below: *Fisherfolk in Cromarty, Scotland, a hundred years ago. In the foreground is a scull.*
Opposite, top: *A frame basket made by Hungarian gypsies; constructed from split black maple on a briar hoop.*
Opposite, centre: *Scottish scull or shook from Ullapool in Wester Ross. Baited long lines with up to 1,400 hooks were coiled into it by fishermen's womenfolk. On occasion, sculls also served as cradles.*

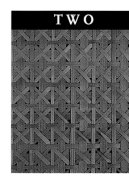

Uses and distribution

Frame basketry is very tough and excellent for transporting heavy items. Single-hoop baskets such as the Welsh willow *cyntell* or the Cumberland swill, made of riven oak strips, are made in several sizes and were once widely used for many tasks, including harvesting vegetables and carrying charcoal.

Common examples of the two-hoop method include the rectangular Southport 'boat' basket which was originally used in England to carry dairy produce and the distinctive 'melon' or 'buttocks' basket, with its bulging double bottom, which was introduced to the USA by European immigrants. Frame baskets made of a number of different materials, notably oak and willow, were once common all over Europe. Gypsies in Hungary still use split black maple and in Poland baskets that will hold water are made from spruce roots and juniper.

In North America the frame technique is most often found in association with oak and ash splints. European colonists took the technique with them to the New World, but it is believed that Native Americans in the North and Southeast also made frame baskets out of splints, willow and basswood.

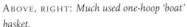

ABOVE, RIGHT: *Much used one-hoop 'boat' basket.*

RIGHT: *Scottish-style buttocks basket for carrying eggs; made by Kay Johnson.*

LINKING AND LOOPING

Linked or looped structures are built up without a passive warp, just an active weft.

Technique

Work begins with a ground weft anchored between two fixed points. The second weft is attached to this in a series of loose loops. Every successive pass of the weft is then looped on to the previous row of loops. Depending on the pliability of the materials and the degree of rigidity required from the finished structure, the loops may be attached to each other in a number of ways. They may simply be threaded through, or fastened with a knot, or threaded through several separate loops in a figure-of-eight pattern.

Fishing nets are built up with a knotted structure, using a shuttle to hold the twine. Finely linked bags are most often constructed with the aid of a needle.

Soft basketry

Baskets and bags of soft fibres such as hemp or agave are used around the world to transport all manner of objects in much the same way as modern Europeans and Americans would use a plastic carrier bag. In New Guinea *bilums* are used to carry food, pigs or even babies. In the Andean mountains of South America bags usually fulfil the role normally taken by baskets. In Ecuador *shigras*, now made for the tourist market, once carried water, while in Colombia a pair of *mochilas*, slung across the chest like bandoliers, are part of the traditional costume of Native Americans such as the Arhuacos who use one for personal items and the other for coca leaves.

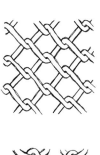

METHODS OF LINKING AND LOOPING

Top: *Bag, from Burundi, in which each thread loops through two others.*
Above, middle: *Looped hemp bag used by the Hani of Yunnan, China.*
Right: *Aboriginal knotted pandanus-fibre bag from Maningrida, Arnhem Land, Australia.*

Hard basketry

I N England the weave employed to make corn dollies creates a simple spiralling structure, with each strand of straw in turn bent over the adjacent one. The same technique is sometimes used in willow work to make rattles, decorative basket walls or details on chair legs.

Wire is also frequently manipulated in this way as, once bent, it will maintain its shape. Linked wire structures are present in salad shakers, strainers and even chicken wire and chainlink fencing.

In the *imbenges* of South Africa, and more recently Zimbabwe, interlinked structures are utilized to achieve the maximum decorative potential from colourful plastic-covered telephone wire.

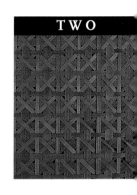

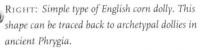

RIGHT: *Simple type of English corn dolly. This shape can be traced back to archetypal dollies in ancient Phrygia.*

BELOW AND BOTTOM: *Hat worn by Muslims and a looped stand acquired in Malaysia.*

ABOVE: A shigra *made from looped maguey (sisal) at Salcedo in Ecuador. These bags were originally used to store food and carry water.*

BELOW: *Two telephone-wire* imbenges. *They were developed by Zulu night watchmen in Johannesburg, South Africa, in the 1980s using recycled materials to imitate traditional forms.*

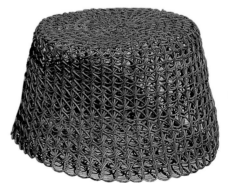

ASSEMBLY

Tʜᴇ definition of a basket usually includes some reference to weaving or interlacing, but there are many items, undeniably baskets, that are either partially or even wholly constructed by other means. These are not only modern creations – in fact, simple assembly techniques, quick and easy to use, may be some of the oldest techniques of all.

Methods of fixing

Bᴀsᴋᴇᴛs of birch or elm bark have been made by the inhabitants of the forests of northern Europe and the USA for millennia. The simplest involve no more than folding the bark into place and securing it with a twig or pine needles. Resin may also be employed to glue the sides together.

Securing separate parts or members may also be accomplished with pegs, nails, rivets or even bolts. The hoop of a frame basket, for example, is frequently nailed into place. Separate elements can be tied in place using twine or wire. Rattan and bamboo furniture, whether from the Philippines or northeast India, is sometimes nailed together, but is usually reinforced with decorative bindings and lashing. The structure may also incorporate simple carpentry techniques with parts slotting into each other.

Baskets of stiff wire such as potato baskets, traps or cages were originally interlaced, but are often welded together, making them virtually indestructible.

Lᴇꜰᴛ: *Bamboo bowl made in the Philippines during the 1950s or 1960s using plaiting, lattice twining and sewing.*

Tᴏᴘ: *A wastepaper basket made in Silchar, Assam, India. This method of creating rigidity with two opposing diagonals is traditionally used to make stools and stands not only in India, but also in the Amazon jungle and amongst the Apache of New Mexico and Arizona.*
Aʙᴏᴠᴇ: *Cages for song birds are found all over the world. Many, like this one from southern Thailand, are assembled using joinery techniques.*

LEFT: *A souvenir, from Crete, constructed from wooden balls threaded on wire.*
BELOW, CENTRE: *French 'trug' for harvesting grapes or artichokes; made from nailed wooden slats.*
BOTTOM LEFT: *Carl Sadler nailing the hoops of a trug, England.*
BOTTOM RIGHT: *A Sussex trug with chestnut hoops and oak slats fixed with copper nails, England.*

TWO

Trugs

ONE notable example of a basket made with assembly techniques is the Sussex trug which derives its name from the Saxon word for boat. Invented in the 1850s in England and widely imitated, it remains popular to this day as a carrier for garden produce. The trug is a frame basket with two hoops of ash or chestnut steamed and bent into shape. The bottom is made from carefully trimmed slats of oak or cricketbat willow that overlap slightly. All the separate pieces are held in place with copper nails.

French equivalents of the trug are made from willow slats nailed together. They are used for harvesting Jerusalem artichokes and grapes.

OPENWORK

Aɴʏ technique may be employed to construct an openwork basket – all that is required is that the weaving elements are more widely spaced. To maintain the integrity of this kind of structure either rims and edges must be reinforced with more tightly packed work, or the materials must be fairly rigid. In openwork baskets made, for example, using the stake and strand method, fitching and pairing are employed more than randing.

An open structure can be a positive advantage in many situations as it allows the passing of air, light and water, but nothing over a certain size.

Aʙᴏᴠᴇ: *Fishing baskets in Madagascar.*
Lᴇꜰᴛ: *A French* panier à jour*; the stakes are held in place with fitching.*
Bᴇʟᴏᴡ: Sciathógs, *Irish potato sieves, made by Alison Fitzgerald.*

Economy

Iɴ societies where baskets are used for everyday tasks, many are made with an open weave purely for economy. It is quicker to weave an open structure and saves valuable time. Materials may also be hard to acquire or expensive. An open structure saves on materials and cost, and also on weight.

Sieves

Sɪᴇᴠᴇs and strainers are used all over the world to grade objects by size (for instance, Japanese shiitake mushroom sieves), to wash, rinse or drain food (the Irish *sciathóg* for draining potatoes) or to separate dross (the English garden and agricultural riddle). An open container which allows the passing of air will ensure that food stays fresh.

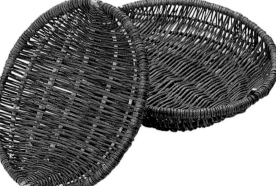

Traps

TRAPS are normally made with an open structure. Air or water can pass through and the hunter can see in, but the victim cannot escape. An enormous variety of traps exists for capturing different species of eels, fish and crustaceans, both marine and fresh water. Animals prized for their pelts, pests and vermin are also caught in traps. In England, before the widespread use of poisons as a form of pest control, wire traps in various designs were employed to catch rats, mice, moles, weasels and any other creature that offended the farmer.

Cages

MANY animals awaiting the cooking pot or a trip to market are kept in cages. Whether made of wire, willow or bamboo, the prisoner requires light and air to remain healthy. Cages for pets, particularly birds, are more elaborate and may become fantastic concoctions. In Tunisia songbirds are kept in wire extravaganzas with minarets and domes, while in southern Thailand competitive singing doves are sometimes kept in cages worth thousands of pounds!

TOP: Panier périgourdin; *a traditional openwork willow basket, from southwest France, made by Norbert Fauré.*
ABOVE, LEFT: *Split-cane fishtrap from the Indonesian island of Lombok.*

ABOVE, RIGHT: *An Aboriginal openwork twined pandanus dilly bag from Kowanyama, Gulf of Carpentaria, Northern Queensland, Australia.*

BASES

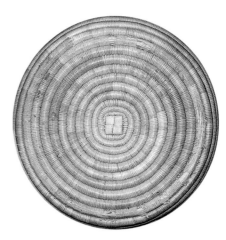

W ITH very few exceptions, the base is the starting-point of a basket and provides a solid foundation on which it is built and upon which it must stand. Subtle differences in the way baskets are begun can also give the initiated clues as to their precise origin. Does a coiled basket begin with a tapered coil or with a knot? Does a stake and strand basket start with a slath or a star?

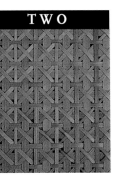

Solid bases

B OTH coiled and stake and strand baskets may be begun with a solid starter piece with holes drilled around the edges. It is usually wood, as in the case of Swedish fish baskets, but Alaskan Eskimos developed a coiled baleen basket during the twentieth century that employed starter pieces made from walrus ivory for the base and lid. Drilled wood bases were widely used in mid-twentieth-century Europe by both amateur and professional craftsmen. They were also used by men making baskets to pass the time during long tours of duty on the Nantucket lightships which sailed from 1854 to 1905 in the dangerous waters between New York and Boston.

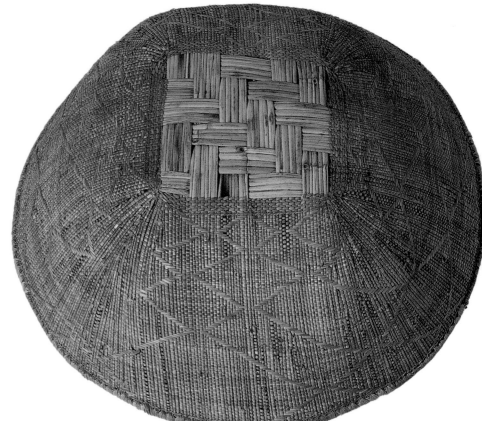

ABOVE: *A bowl, from Latvia, with a drilled birch bark base and sides constructed with white willow coils. The stitching is split willow.*

TOP: *A coiled Ovambo basket, from Namibia, showing the four-square knot with which it was begun.*
ABOVE: *Grain basket from Zambia. It has a twilled stake and strand structure started with a square base of twill-plaited split cane.*
LEFT: *A coiled basket, or hat, from California or the USA's Southwest, started with a tight spiral.*

Feet

To give a basket stability or to raise it off the ground, a number of methods may be used to make feet. In a stake and strand basket this may involve inserting extra rods into the base and working a wale downwards as well as up. Bowl-shaped baskets may be intended for manual use and not be required to be freestanding, but should they need to stand, a ring can be constructed separately and sewn to the base to make it stable.

In Asia baskets for carrying or for storage sometimes have a long rod woven vertically into each corner or attached to the outside. They reinforce the basket and project beyond the base to provide feet, and may be reinforced with strips of wood shaped into a square or ring.

In Southeast Asia pots for storing and carrying cooked rice are fitted with a foot made from two pieces of wood slotted together in a cross and stitched to the base. In northeastern Thailand *kong khao*, containers for sticky rice, may be fitted with a slotted foot of exaggerated proportions and often have a complementary shape fitted to the lid.

Stands

Feet or stands can be constructed as items to be used independently. A stiff material such as bamboo can be woven into a ring on which a round-bottomed cooking pot such as a karai or wok can be placed. It might also be employed as a base for a steamer in a pan of hot water.

Top: A Congolese stake and strand basket with bamboo feet. A spur is left when the bamboo is cut so that it can be woven into the basket.

Top right: A fisherman's basket, from Lombok, Indonesia, raised on a base of wooden slats.

Above: Balinese bamboo storage basket standing on a plaited ring attached with synthetic twine. The lid is missing.

Left: Coiled Moroccan bowl inverted to show how the foot was constructed separately and attached after completion.

Right: Finnish pot stand made from strips of birch bark; a temporary base.

RIMS

TWO

THE rim is one of the most vulnerable parts of any basket as it is subject to a great deal of wear and tear. It is here that most weaves are completed and loose ends must be secured to prevent unravelling and to protect the hands of the user. Many baskets also depend on a strong border to maintain their shape.

Baskets with no border

A FEW baskets such as the Irish donkey creel have an unfinished appearance as the tops of the stakes are left exposed. Frame baskets, on the other hand, have an even edge as the strands are woven back and forth over the frames during construction.

Integrated rims

PLAITED and stake and strand baskets are normally finished by threading the loose ends back down into the weave of the walls. A strong rim is created by working a border. To do this the stakes are bent over and interwoven or plaited together around the rim before being cut off short or threaded down into the basket wall. French braid or rope borders provide a strong and attractive finish. Trac weave, also called a Madeira, or, in France,

Monaco border, creates a basket with no loose ends as one element of the interweaving consists of the stakes as they travel diagonally up, and the other consists of the same stakes, bent over, as they travel diagonally back down to the base.

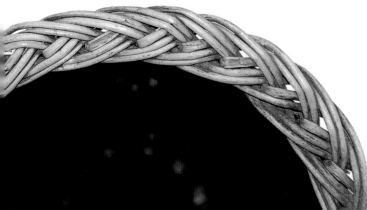

ABOVE, LEFT: *A woman carrying a frame basket and a burden basket with exposed stakes, Newhaven, Scotland.*
LEFT: *A plaited border on an English egg basket.*

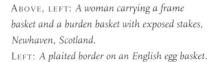

TOP: *Selling fish from a frame basket with an integrated rim, Cromarty, Scotland.*
ABOVE: *Twill-plaited container from the Democratic Republic of Congo. The rims of both lid and base are reinforced with strips of wood carved in low relief.*

This technique is particularly common in Mediterranean countries, but is also used in the Philippines and New Mexico.

Coiled baskets are generally completed by tapering the thickness of the coil so that the ending is not so obvious. The Hopi of Arizona use this method, except when making plaques for a newborn baby or bridegroom, where the coil of galleta grass is cut off abruptly. A coiled basket may also be finished with a decorative edging created by fixing the final turn of the coil in an openwork zigzag. Many coiled and twined baskets are completed with a strong rim worked in herringbone stitch or false braid resembling a plait. This is often worked in a contrasting colour for decorative effect.

Reinforced rims

ANOTHER strong rim, particularly common on plaited baskets such as sifters and winnowing trays, involves tightly binding the edge between two slats of cane, bamboo or wood splint that grip it like a vice. Today, stitching is often carried out with strips of synthetic fibres.

ABOVE: *Turkish coiled bowl in which the final coil is attached as zigzags.*
BELOW: *Nigerian palm-fibre pot cover finished with a looped rim.*

ABOVE: *Moroccan esparto grass bowl with a herringbone or false braid rim.*
BELOW: *Trac weave border on a cocorib basket from the Philippines.*
BOTTOM, LEFT: *Ghanaian children in Accra learning how to work the rim of a twined grass basket.*

HANDLES

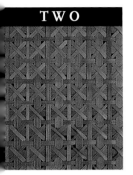

THE addition of handles makes a basket more portable. They may be an integral part of the structure from an early stage or they may be added to an otherwise completed basket. The number of handles and their positioning is determined by the basket's function.

Integral handles

THE solid hoops of frame baskets make strong handles. With a single hoop a gap is left on each side to provide an opening into which a hand may be inserted. When two hoops are used, the vertical one rises above the rim to create the handle. The point of intersection may be reinforced with interlacing worked into a decorative lozenge sometimes referred to as a 'God's eye'.

ABOVE: *A skeined willow 'hen basket' made in the Former Yugoslavia.*

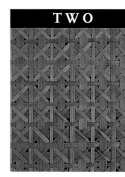

The 'hen' basket is a classic and widely used design constructed from a set of adjacent vertical hoops spaced more widely at the bottom. The structural hoops are all bound together at the top to make the handle.

Most coiled baskets lack handles. When they are required loops can be created by pulling the progressing coil material out from the body of the basket for a short distance.

Added handles

WHEN handles are added after the construction of the body of a stake and strand basket they must be attached securely. The strongest method involves pushing one end of a sharpened rod into the basket's walls beside a stake, bending it over at the top and pushing the other end in beside another stake. This loop is then wrapped with flexible rods threaded below the rim and then twisted back and forth around the foundation rod.

OPPOSITE: Plaited bamboo baskets, from Nepal, with handles bound to the rims.
OPPOSITE, INSET: Making the handle for a Ghanaian twined grass basket.
RIGHT: Bread mat from eastern Turkey. The final coil forms a loop.
FAR RIGHT: Twined basket from Huacho, Peru, with added handles.

To guarantee a secure handle the rim must be tight and strong, particularly if the handle, as is the case with many twined baskets, is attached directly to the rim. If the rim is weak a load pulling against the handle could pull the basket apart.

Straps

FOR soft baskets and bags constructed from coiled plaits, or by plaiting, or by linking and looping, flexible straps are preferable. These may be threaded through the basket and knotted or sewn on. Stake and strand and twined baskets sometimes have straps secured with rivets. Leather straps are common, but many baskets and bags are fitted with fibre cords or braids, often plaited in ingenious patterns.

ABOVE, LEFT: Mediterranean frame basket with an eccentric handle.
TOP RIGHT: European-style frame basket made of rattan. One hoop forms the handle.
ABOVE: 'Flour' basket from Shanxi province in the north of China. The handles are made of wooden slats which are notched to allow secure attachment to the rim.

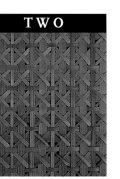

To keep their contents safe and clean many baskets have lids. These may well be treated as a decorative feature and be far more elaborate than is functionally necessary.

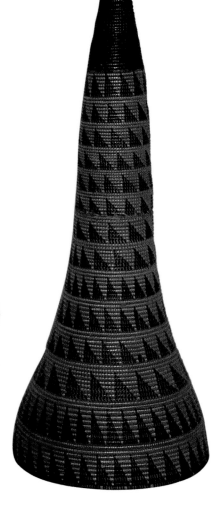

Covers

THE simplest lids are flat coiled mats like those used in Saharan and sub-saharan Africa to cover earthenware water jars and keep out dust and insects. They are not attached to the jar in any way. The Zulus in South Africa traditionally make bowl-shaped coiled *imbenges* which are inverted over the tops of the clay pots in which sorghum-based beer is brewed and stored. In Mali and Niger pot covers are decorated with striking abstract and figurative patterns in black, rust and natural colours.

Lids that fit over a basket

PERHAPS the simplest way of making a fitted lid is to construct a shallow basket with a slightly greater diameter than the basket over which it is inverted. Coiled, plaited, twined and wicker lids can all be made in this way. One interesting example of this method is the brightly dyed *sikki* grass baskets made around Mithila in the Indian state of Bihar. The conical lid fits over a lip fitted within the rim of the basket.

Lids that fit inside a basket

THE tightest fitting lids act like stoppers. They are made to overlap the basket slightly and have on their underside a single coil or ring with a marginally smaller diameter than the opening of the basket. Coiled pots of this type are widely used, particularly by women, as sewing baskets or for storing personal items. The wool-stitched pots of Berber women in Morocco can fit so tightly that considerable force is sometimes required to prise the lid off.

It is also feasible to construct a lip inside the basket, below the rim, so that the lid may be dropped in.

ABOVE, LEFT: *Coiled sikki grass baskets from Bihar, India. The lid fits over a rim in the base.*
ABOVE: *Lid for a gourd, containing banana wine, made from coiled grass by the Tutsi of Bukoba, Tanzania (27 cm, 11 in. high).*
BELOW, LEFT: *Zulu pot, from South Africa, constructed from coiled grass and ilala palm. The lid fits like a stopper.*
BELOW: *Coiled box from Lombok, Indonesia, with a wooden starter piece.*

Hinged lids

THE lids of items such as picnic baskets, storage hampers, carrier-pigeon crates or sewing baskets generally have hinged lids secured with a clasp or peg. The hinge, or hinges, may be constructed from a loop of twine, wire, leather or fibres that match the fabric of the basket. Expensive and important containers may have hinges and clasps constructed from leather straps secured with rivets.

ABOVE: *The cover for an earthenware water jar; from Mali or the Republic of Niger. It is made of coiled palm ribs stitched with strips of palm leaf. Similar items are in use in subsaharan countries anywhere from Cameroon to the Sudan.*

RIGHT: *A willow picnic basket, made in southern Turkey, fitted with two lids hinged at the handle.*

DECORATION

OPPOSITE:
*Decorated baskets
from around the
world.*
ABOVE, LEFT:
*Pakistani imitation
of a Pima bowl.*
ABOVE, RIGHT:
Bowl from Botswana.
FAR LEFT: *Plaited
pot, Sabah, Malaysia.*
NEAR LEFT: *Javanese
basket for cooked rice.*

DECORATION

THREE

EXAMPLES of all types of basketry, even objects in constant use that might reasonably be left plain or only sparsely patterned, can be found with decoration. Some methods of decorating a basket are very complex, but others are simple. If, at the beginning of the weaving process, some thought is given to layout and materials, a technique such as plaiting needs little subsequent development – the pattern virtually weaves itself.

In traditional societies, it is the baskets made for personal use that have always had the most effort lavished upon them. Baskets that are used for spiritual or ceremonial functions are woven with particular care, often incorporating prescribed colours and designs. They may be used at a coming of age ceremony or a wedding and then treated as an heirloom.

STRUCTURE AND PATTERN

THE restrictions imposed by the structural elements of a basket make particular designs and motifs easier to work and consequently those patterns are the ones that occur most frequently, cropping up independently in isolated locations. Twined baskets often feature bars and diagonals, plaited baskets often feature checks and coiled baskets often feature triangles.

PATTERN AND SOCIAL IDENTITY

THE materials, and therefore the techniques, available to any community may restrict the decorative choices, but motifs of specific significance – reflecting lifestyle, spiritual attitudes and clan allegiances – are a common feature of basketry and are often helpful in identifying origin such as the monkeys or jaguars on basketry in the Amazon rain forest. It is also true that, while many motifs are worked deliberately to resemble something significant, others are developed from the limitations of the techniques and are then given names reflecting their incidental similarities to familiar things – for instance, the 'pigeon's eye' motif on plaited baskets from Sarawak.

Considering the antiquity of basketmaking, it is arguable that patterns like these are the oldest in the world.

OPPOSITE, TOP LEFT: *Ghanaian twined baskets.*
OPPOSITE, ABOVE, RIGHT: *Wounaan twilled boxes, Panama.*
OPPOSITE, LEFT: *Making a Ghanaian grass basket.*
OPPOSITE, BOTTOM: *Decoratively stitched basket from an unidentified former British colony.*

ABOVE, LEFT: *Dyed reeds in the Nigerian town of Ilorin which is situated in Yorubaland.*
TOP, RIGHT: *Dyed savannah grass, intended for basketmaking, laid out to dry in Accra, Ghana.*
ABOVE: *Basketmakers in Madagascar displaying goods twill-plaited from zozoro sedge.*
BELOW: *A brightly dyed coiled plait mat made in Madagascar.*

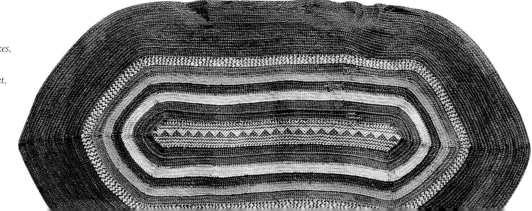

TEXTURE

NATURE provides the basketmaker with a limited palette of colours, but it is still possible to create pattern and decoration with texture, even when using only one type of fibre. The structure of virtually all baskets remains visible, each technique resulting in its own surface texture. By varying the materials or the way in which they are manipulated, many different effects can be achieved.

ABOVE: *Porcupine twist basket made by the Abnaki of the northeast USA.*
LEFT: *Zulu grass mat. Wefts split the plied warps to resemble twining.*
BELOW, LEFT: *Buri palm box, from the Philippines, with twisted decoration on the lid.*
BELOW: *Birch bark basket with a twist in the plaiting, from Archangel, Russia.*
OPPOSITE, LEFT: *Ifugao storage pot from the Philippines. The body of the basket is plaited, while the top is coiled.*
OPPOSITE, RIGHT: *Japanese flower-arranging vase. The texture is created with bamboo splints interlaced on the surface of the basket.*

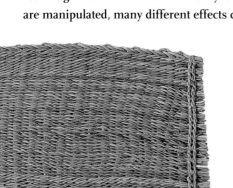

Materials

THERE is a vast difference between the hard, glossy surface of a length of bamboo and the hairiness of a strand of sisal. Materials are frequently chosen because of their texture. Variety can also be achieved by selecting one surface of a splint rather than the other, according to which faced the outside of the plant and was therefore, as in the case of bamboos and rattan, smoothest. Contrast can also be achieved by weaving rods with their bark attached in combination with others that have been stripped.

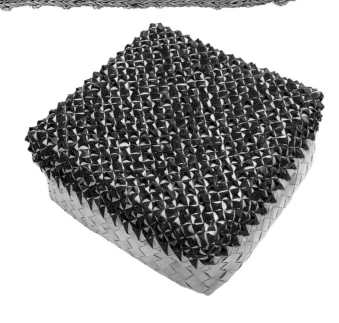

Variation in weave

Varying the way in which the elements of a basket are interwoven creates new textures. The classic form of a willow stake and strand basket with waling, randing, fitching and border is full of texture. Staggering the twill of plaited or stake and strand baskets, even without the use of added colour, will produce a pattern of zigzags, chevrons or lozenges emphasized by the play of light. On the other hand, simply changing the direction of the twist will produce a pattern in a piece of twining such as a Fulani hat or Hawaiian vine basket.

Special effects

Some techniques take elements of a basket out of their structural context and force them into relief. One example of this is the curlicue or porcupine twist baskets made by the Algonquian Indians of the northeastern USA where an overlaid strip is given a twist between each of the stakes that hold it in place. The same technique is traditionally employed in Thailand to decorate baskets in which gifts are presented to priests.

Some baskets may have extra elements inserted into their weave which alter their surface, often at a diagonal. These extra strips or splints may or may not be of the same material as the rest of the basket.

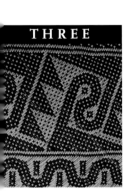

NATURAL COLOURS

THE vast majority of baskets are subtle and subdued, depending on the natural hues of their raw materials for their colour. Ranging from white to the darkest brown, natural colours coexist harmoniously and mellow to warm, golden tones.

Through careful selection and treatment, it is possible to maximize the potential of any given species. *Yucca elata* leaves, for example, can be split, the outer layers providing green fibre and the inner layers almost white.

THREE

TOP LEFT: *Navajo wedding basket; the white is bleached yucca, the red is banana yucca root and the black is devil's claw.*

TOP RIGHT: *A Samoan pandanus hand bag. The pattern is emphasized with natural variations in the colouring of the fibres.*

ABOVE: *A pair of Ovambo baskets from Namibia. Two natural, contrasting colours have been used to create a simple, but striking, design.*

LEFT: *Pima basket from southern Arizona. The fret pattern worked in devil's claw against a background of willow is typical of Pima basketry.*

Preparation

THE way in which materials are prepared can also affect their colour, willow being a supreme example. In their natural state willow rods bear the colour of their bark which is most often brown, but, according to variety, may be yellow, green or even purple. When the bark is stripped, the rods are virtually white. If, however, the rods are boiled or steamed with their bark intact, once stripped they are revealed as buff.

Many plants, including leaves and grasses, may be exposed in the sun or dipped in chemicals to bleach them. Time and use, however, will reduce the whiteness to soft creams or yellows.

Sheen and patina

THE nature of the use to which a basket is put will affect its colouration. Constant contact with greasy hands will impart sheen, but cooking utensils exposed to water and steam will become pale and dull.

In the hills of Indochina bamboo and rattan baskets often have a dark patina achieved through exposure to smoke – the traditional way to prevent insect damage. A sheen is imparted on basketry in parts of Indonesia by deliberately rubbing with coconut oil.

RIGHT: Panier ovale à jour, *a traditional French-style basket made by renowned English basketmaker, David Drew. The contrasting tones of brown and white willow are further enhanced with* Salix purpurea x daphnoides, *one of the many varieties of beautifully coloured willows.*
BELOW: *Ethiopian twined bag made from naturally coloured plant fibres.*

Vibrant natural colours

Plants endowed with naturally vibrant colours are particularly prized by basketmakers. The brilliant red used in Navajo wedding baskets is traditionally provided by roots of the banana yucca, *Yucca arizonica*. Reds and yellows can be obtained right across the northern hemisphere from the stems of dogwoods, *Cornus sp.* One of the plants most valued by the Native Americans of the American Southwest is the devil's claw, *Martynia parviflora*, which produces horned seedpods with black fibres extensively employed in pattern making to contrast with light willow or yucca.

99

DYES

Sᴏᴍᴇ would argue that the beauty and harmony of the colours produced by nature are beyond compare, but many have been unable to resist the temptation to produce a wider man-made palette and expand the possibilities of pattern making.

Natural dyes

Oᴛʜᴇʀ than bleaching in the sun, the simplest method of changing the colour of plant fibres, a process still in evidence in the Amazon basin and central Africa, is to bury them in the ground until they have turned brown. An added bonus of this is that the chemicals naturally present in some soils may also act as a mordant, making the colour surprisingly fast.

THREE

The experience of many generations has provided basketmakers all around the world with the knowledge of which leaves, roots, berries or bark can be boiled up to produce which colour. The local availability of dye plants has therefore dictated the colouring of baskets and become a factor in their identification. In Kenya, for example, loganberries and bougainvillaea flowers are used to make purple and lavender, the Hupa of northern California made a yellow dye from the bark of the Oregon grape, *Berberis nervosa*,

Aʙᴏᴠᴇ, ʟᴇꜰᴛ: *Detail of a mat from Madagascar.*
Aʙᴏᴠᴇ: *Coiled basket from Uganda.*
Bᴇʟᴏᴡ, ʟᴇꜰᴛ: *Hopi coiled plaque from Second Mesa, Arizona, USA. The grass coils have been stitched with yucca fibre tinted with natural dyes.*

Aʙᴏᴠᴇ: *Coiled pot, from Yemen, stitched with natural and dyed fibres.*
Bᴇʟᴏᴡ: *Plaited* yarumo-*fibre basket from Vaupes, Colombia. The fibres are dyed with tree sap or clay.*

RIGHT: Bundle-coiled eating tray from Ethiopia or the Sudan. Sunshine has mellowed the bright, artificial dyes.

in Sarawak mats are sometimes made from rattan dyed with indigo, while in Colombia palm fibres are dyed red with the seeds of the *achiote* tree.

Synthetic dyes

ANILINE dyes were developed from coal tar in the nineteenth century and provided an easy method of dyeing textiles and yarn virtually any colour. These dyes, much quicker to use than natural dyes, were enthusiastically adopted for dyeing cloth and basketmaking materials all over the world.

Academics and collectors often regard subdued natural colours as being more authentic and traditional, and purists have frequently frowned upon the use of synthetic dyes as a 'debasement' of traditional culture. But tradition is a living thing and the enthusiasm with

BELOW, LEFT: Coiled plait basket, from Mexico, made from palm fibre dyed with synthetic dye.
BELOW, RIGHT: A Malay ceremonial basket of brightly dyed fibres.

which basketmakers have embraced the use of vivid pigments reveals an innate love of bright colour that was previously thwarted by the limitations of natural dyes. Of course, rampant exuberance has led at times to some garish results.

APPLIED COLOUR

THE process of treating raw materials with dyes is carried out before weaving can begin, but colour can be applied to the surface of a basket using paint or pigment either before or after construction. Compared to the time-consuming complexities of pattern weaving, the act of painting on a design, whether decorative, magical or as a mark of the owner's identity, is a simple task.

Most often pigments are applied with some form of brush, but the distinctive splint baskets of the Mohegan of Connecticut were decorated with designs printed on with a stamp cut from a potato.

Weaving and painting

COLOUR is frequently applied over the surface of basketry with complete disregard for the texture of the weaving. The magnificent twined spruce-root hats made by women of the Haida and Tlingit in the American Northwest have beautiful twill-twined patterns which are overlaid with totemic animal motifs painted by their menfolk. Conversely, some painting appears to be incorporated into the weaving as in the case of Western Apache burden baskets, although the paint is actually applied after weaving – to one stitch at a time with great care and precision.

Homemade pigment

PEOPLE have always depended upon locally available materials to make their pigments just as much as their dyes. Commonplace substances such as lampblack or soot make an easy-to-apply black colouring when mixed with oil. The by-products of basketmaking may also be exploited, as in Borneo where the berries of the rattan plant are boiled to release a waxy red substance that can be applied with a stick. This paste was sold in medieval Europe under the mysterious name 'dragon's blood'.

Commercial pigment

THE European colonization of much of the world led to the wider availability of factory-made products such as paint. Bright, easy to apply and long lasting, commercial products were eagerly adopted by many basketmakers who considered the time saved in the preparation of pigments well worth the expense. Colours became available in tins or bottles that could not be made from local materials.

Paint itself is not the only source of pigment exploited by enterprising basketmakers, people well practised at improvising. Other commercial products applied to baskets include boot polish, ink and fibre-tip pens.

ABOVE, LEFT: *Plaited Iban hat painted with 'dragon's blood', Borneo.*
LEFT: *Painted basket, from the Swedish province of Hälsingland, used to carry gifts of food to weddings and funerals.*
OPPOSITE: *Basket, from Kalimantan, with splints painted before plaiting.*

ABOVE: *A Balinese keben plaited from strips split from the inside of a bamboo culm; used for storing valued possessions.*
BELOW: *Karen plaited box, from Myanmar (Burma), decorated with painted motifs; used by the Karen hill tribe for storing medicine or magical objects.*

THREE

TLINGIT PAINTED
SPRUCE-ROOT HAT

RESIN

IT takes time and great skill to construct a basket that will hold water. It is simpler to coat its surfaces with clay or resin. The Native Americans of the American Southwest, for example, coated some of their baskets with pitch collected from the piñon tree, *Pinus edulis*, to render them waterproof. The application of resin will also protect a basket from mould or infestation.

Lacquer

THE use of resins was perfected in ancient China, using sap from a type of sumac, *Rhus vernicifera*, known as the lac tree. The techniques spread to Japan with the dissemination of Buddhism in the sixth century AD and reached the height of sophistication during the Japanese Edo period. Lacquer can be applied to any smooth surface – wood, textile, leather or ceramic – and exquisite pots can be created by applying lacquer to the surface of a woven bamboo basket.

The bark of a lac tree is cut with a diagonal slash so that the sap will bleed and run down the cut. The sap is collected in a cup at the bottom, just as in the harvesting of rubber, and then purified by boiling and straining it.

ABOVE: *A split bamboo dowry box, made by Sankhari women in the Indian state of Orissa, coated with 'Indian lac'.*
LEFT: *Navajo water jar coiled from bundles of willow splints and coated inside and out with piñon pitch, Canon de Chelly, Arizona, USA.*
BELOW, LEFT: *Plaited bamboo pot coated in lacquer and paint from Myanmar (Burma).*
BELOW: *Stacking lacquered container for betel nut and accessories made by members of the Karen hill tribe in northern Thailand. The foundation is bamboo stake and strand basketry.*
OPPOSITE, ABOVE, LEFT: *Lacquer-coated bamboo rice container from northern Thailand. Chiang Mai is the centre of Thai lacquerware production.*

The surface to be lacquered needs to be as smooth as possible and may therefore be boiled and scrupulously rubbed down. Any imperfections can be filled by smearing the surface with some form of paste.

As many as twelve coats of lacquer are then painted on, allowing each layer to dry completely in a clean atmosphere before the following coat is applied. The whole process can therefore take as long as three weeks. Dried in a moist atmosphere, the lacquer forms a tough, heat and solvent resistant surface that can be polished to a brilliant sheen.

Painted decoration may be applied either under or over the layers of lacquer.

Distribution

Lacquerware is widely produced in China and Japan, but mostly on surfaces other than baskets. In Vietnam, Myanmar (Burma) and Thailand bamboo baskets lacquered with resin from the *rak* tree, *Melanorrhoea usitata*, are used to serve food and to store cooked rice. Burmese cylindrical pots and bowls, decorated with paint and lacquer over a tightly woven base, have become a popular export item in recent years.

In the Indian state of Orissa, dowry boxes are coated with 'Indian' or 'sind' lac, which is a gummy secretion extruded by the lac beetle, *Coccus lacca*. Shellac is a varnish refined from this resin and is used in Europe and the USA to stiffen and waterproof straw hats.

ABOVE: *Lacquered tiffin basket from Fukien, China. Bands of the basketry foundation have been left visible.*
RIGHT: *Rice container, from Vietnam, partly lacquered over plaited bamboo.*

O N a coiled basket the stitching and binding are the dominant decorative features. The impression they make can be emphasized by their spacing, their relationship with each other, their colour or their length.

Spacing

T HE stitching that holds the coils together frequently covers the entire surface of a basket, but structural integrity can be maintained if the stitches are spaced out. This can provide an interesting contrast between the texture of the coil material and the stitches. Patterns can also be built up by carefully aligning the stitches in a number of ways. Variations

THREE

TOP: *Spaced stitching on Papago baskets from Arizona.*

ABOVE, LEFT: *Tight raffia stitching on a Ugandan bowl.*

ABOVE, RIGHT: *Long stitches on a sikki grass bowl from Bihar, India.*

LEFT: *Coiled bowls, from Bangladesh, stitched with dyed palm fibre.*

OPPOSITE, TOP RIGHT: *Wrapped coils on a palm basket from India, which create an open structure.*

OPPOSITE, ABOVE, LEFT: *Bowl, from Yemen, decorated with stitching in different colours.*

OPPOSITE, BELOW, LEFT: *Palm-fibre basket, from Sonora, Mexico, with wrapped coils and spaced stitching.*

OPPOSITE, BELOW, RIGHT: *Bundle-coiled tray with a design created by varying the length of the stitches; possibly from the Baltic.*

on this technique using beargrass with yucca stitching are a speciality of the Papago (now called Tohono O'odham) of southern Arizona who are among the most prolific basketmakers in the USA today.

Splitting

STITCHES may be placed beside those in previous coils or interlinked to create a smooth surface. However, for a subtle decorative effect, a stitch may deliberately split or bifurcate the one below. Exponents of this can be found in South Africa and Sweden and among the Mapuche Indians in Chile.

Wrapping

IN between spaced stitches the coils are often wrapped to conceal their fibres and to achieve a uniform surface. The stitches may also be twisted and knotted, forcing a gap between coils and so creating an openweave. Countries where baskets with this structure are made include India, Pakistan, Portugal and Mexico.

Length

NORMALLY a stitch is used to sew one coil to the previous one, but by extending the stitch over several coils exciting textures can be created. Good examples of this technique are to be found in Ethiopia and, notably, the Indian state of Bihar.

Colour

PERIODICALLY changing the colour of the fibre used for stitching and wrapping is the most common method of pattern making in coiled basketry. The variety of designs that have been produced is staggering, ranging from the geometric to the symbolic and figurative. Arrangements of triangles, stars and zigzags are the most widespread of all motifs.

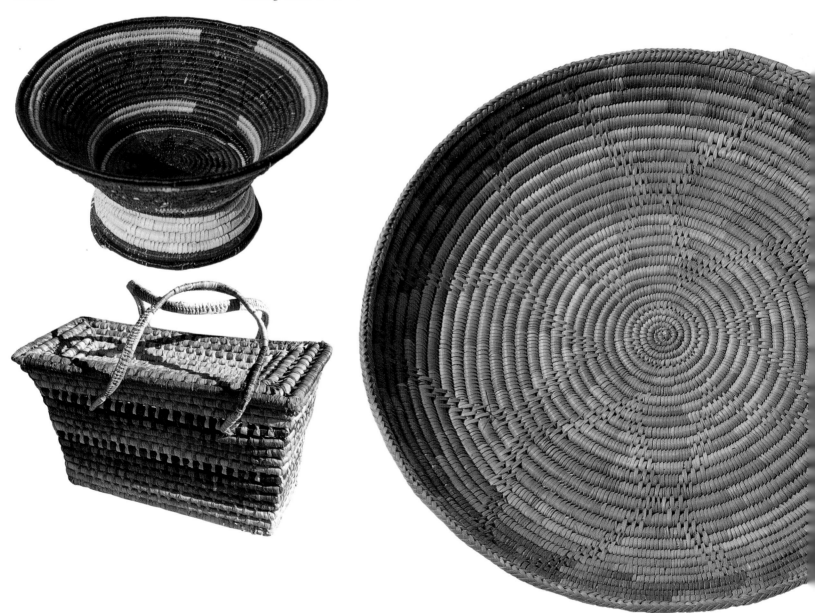

IMBRICATION AND BEADING

TOP DRAWING:
EGYPTIANS
HARVESTING FIGS IN
IMBRICATED BASKETS,
AFTER A PAINTING
IN THE TOMB OF
KHNUMHOTEP AT
BENI HASAN,
C. 1950 BC

DERIVED from the Latin word *imbricare*, which means 'to overlap like roof tiles', imbrication can refer to the texture of a snake's skin or a method of making a distinctive surface texture on coiled baskets. Now the technique is most often associated with spruce or cedar root baskets, overlaid with coloured grass or cherry bark, which are made by Thompson River Indians and other Salish speakers from British Columbia and Washington State in the American Northwest. These baskets are sometimes referred to as 'Klikitat', although strictly speaking this applies to tall baskets with looped rims made by the 'warrior' Klikitat who lived in the Columbia River area of Washington State.

Imbricated baskets were also made in Ancient Egypt using palm leaves. In the tomb of Khnumhotep at Beni Hasan, which dates back to around 1950 BC, there is a wall painting of two men picking figs and packing them into what appear to be imbricated baskets. The craft survives today in only a few villages in New Nubia, an area north of Aswan.

Technique

DURING the process of sewing coils together a strip of grass or bark is attached to the surface. The strip is folded back on itself and secured with a binding stitch. It is then folded over, concealing the stitch, and then repeatedly folded and stitched around the basket to produce the appearance of rectangular blocks overlapping like roof tiles. The stitching is completely hidden.

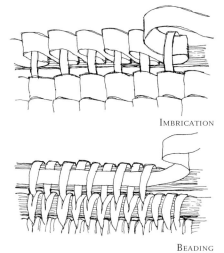

IMBRICATION

BEADING

Beading

A LESS sophisticated technique, known as beading, is much simpler to use and can also be found in the same regions. With this method, a strip is laid flat across the surface of the coil and bound down under the stitches which are spaced to reveal the strip. In the American Northwest grass and bark are again the chosen materials, but in North Africa rags, leather or yarn are more often utilized.

FAR LEFT AND NEAR LEFT, BELOW: *Grain storage basket, from Morocco, with a pattern worked by beading with leather strips; and a detail of the leather beading.*
ABOVE, NEAR LEFT: *Klikitat basket from Washington State, USA. The Cedar or spruce root structure is decorated with imbricated squaw grass,* Xerophyllum tenax.

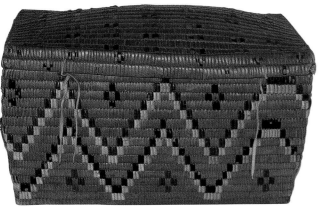

ABOVE: *A basket used by women to hold personal belongings, from Siwa Oasis in northwest Egypt. It is decorated with silk floss tassels and beading in leather and cloth.*

LEFT: *Interior Salish spruce root chest, from British Columbia, Canada, decorated with imbricated strips of grass and cherry bark.*

109

TWILLING

Employed with plaited, twined, or stake and strand baskets, twilling is a simple technique that greatly increases the number of decorative arrangements possible. When using elements of the same colour, subtle patterns can be worked in the surface texture, but when the elements are of different colours, it is possible to work striking figurative or abstract designs.

Twilled basketry may be woven loosely, but when tight it can be more rigid and impenetrable than a plainweave basket.

Technique

The normal practice of interweaving is to interlace elements over one, under one, over one, and so on. However, if the sequence is varied, the even checked layout is broken up. If the arrangement, or twill, is over two, under one (2/1) the staggered repetition in subsequent rows of weaving will create a diagonal pattern. If, after regular intervals, the stagger is reversed, a pattern of lozenges or zigzags will be built up.

Many variations are possible and in some cultures these are given specific names. The Iban of Sarawak, for example, use many twills including *anyam cit padi* (rice mouse weave), *anyam mata puna* (pigeon's eye weave) and *ikoh angkih* (porcupine tail).

LEFT: *Mata punai motif on an Iban basket*

BELOW: 3/3 TWILL

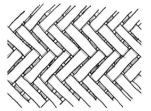

Above, left: *Twill-plaited English chaff riddle.*
Above, right: *Iban rice-reaping basket.*
Below: *A Cherokee basket from North Carolina and a Tarahumara basket from Chihuahua, Mexico.*

Colour

When working with colour, it is usual to have each set of elements composed of a different colour. When one colour is needed in the design it is made to float across the surface, hiding the other colour. When the strands or splints employed are very fine it is possible to work delicate patterns of great complexity, but to maintain structural integrity the floats must not be too long, so large blocks of colour are broken with dots of the other colour.

Uses and distribution

Twilled basketry is to be found all over the world, from chopstick holders and beer strainers to panels for house walls.

ABOVE: *Stretchy, twilled beer or casava strainer bought in Lesotho.*
LEFT: *A seventeenth-century Kongo pot with fine twilled surface pattern, from the Lower Congo.*
BELOW: *Stake and strand Batonga tsero (winnowing tray) with twilled decoration, from Matabeleland, Zimbabwe.*

The restrictions of the colour technique have resulted in a profusion of baskets and mats around the world often bearing a startling similarity to one another. The river cane plaiting of the Chitimacha of Louisiana and the split rattan work of the Dyak of Kalimantan, for instance, both have a different colour for each axis which is made to float at selected intervals. Both seem to have two patterns overlaying each other, one of stripes and one of hooked meandering lines.

THREE

DECORATIVE TWINING

A NUMBER of inventive variations have been developed that make the decorative possibilities of twining extensive.

Three-strand twining

THIS technique is virtually the same as the stake and strand technique of waling, and gives extra strength to a twined weave. By using a contrasting colour for one strand, it is possible to build up a design of spaced diagonals.

Crossed-warp twining

EMPLOYED by the Makah of Washington State and the indigenous inhabitants of the Aleutian Islands, crossed-warp twining uses a pair of warps that cross each other on the diagonal and a pair of twining wefts that bind them together. This produces an openwork structure often combined with solid plain twining.

CROSSED-WARP
TWINING

Wrap or wrapped twining

INTRICATELY patterned bowls, pots and hats are made by the Nootka of British Columbia, often with designs depicting whaling scenes. These are created using a technique known as wrapped twining in which one stiff weft and one flexible weft are used. The stiff one is laid across the warps and then bound down by the flexible one. The inside of the basket resembles coiling, but the outside has the distinctive diagonal twist of twining.

WRAP
TWINING

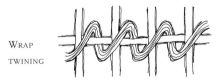

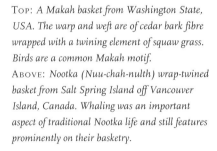

TOP: *A Makah basket from Washington State, USA. The warp and weft are of cedar bark fibre wrapped with a twining element of squaw grass. Birds are a common Makah motif.*
ABOVE: *Nootka (Nuu-chah-nulth) wrap-twined basket from Salt Spring Island off Vancouver Island, Canada. Whaling was an important aspect of traditional Nootka life and still features prominently on their basketry.*

Lattice or T-twining

LATTICE or T-twining is constructed in the same way as wrap twining, but employs a pair of twining wefts. Lattice twining is often found on the grain baskets of southern Africa and the twined baskets of the Pomo of California.

LATTICE
TWINING

THREE

Overlay

IN northern California, baskets were often decorated by laying a strip of coloured beargrass or fern stem along the conifer root wefts and weaving them in. When given a full twist, the pattern appears on both sides, but a half twist will only show the colour on the outside.

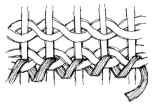

FALSE EMBROIDERY

False embroidery

WHEN building up a plain twined structure, a decorative strand of wool or coloured grass can be wrapped around each twining weft as it appears on the surface. This creates a pattern on the outside surface only which seems to slant in the opposite direction to the plain twined areas. This technique was perfected by the Tlingit and Aleutian Islanders of the American Northwest and the Nez Perce of the Plateau.

BELOW, LEFT: *Set of glass holders, from the Aleutian Islands, made from beach rye grass,* Elymus mollis, *in crossed warp twining.*
BELOW, RIGHT: *A finely twined basket, from the Aleutian Islands, with motifs worked in false embroidery. The swastika appears globally as a solar, good luck symbol.*

WRAP-TWINED HAT WORN BY MAQUINA A NUU-CHAH-NULTH (NOOTKA) CHIEF, AFTER A DRAWING OF 1792

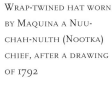

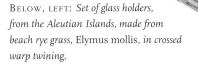

Mᴀɴʏ baskets are constructed using a mixture of materials for different parts of their structure as some parts must be strong and others flexible. For instance, a coiled English bee skep may have bundled straw for its foundation, stitched together with split bramble stems, whereas a Cumberland swill would have a hazel rim and oak slats. However, the decision to use a mixture of materials may be purely aesthetic and intended to produce decorative contrasts. Mixing can involve colour, texture or both.

Mixing colours

Cᴏɴᴛʀᴀsᴛɪɴɢ colours can be achieved without dyeing by simply selecting a variety of fibres with appropriate colouration. In a plaited structure using different-coloured fibres of the same size for each axis creates an immediate pattern. In northeast India, for example, the contrasting materials might be light bamboo and dark rattan. The different design motifs of a Washo coiled basket from Nevada might require willow for white, redbud bark for red and fern root for black.

Mixing textures

Tʜᴇ contrasting effects created by texture can be most striking. Using materials with different diameters will produce interesting corrugations, but the most fascinating combinations are those that exploit different surfaces, whether it be the lustrous sheen of bamboo, the sponginess of rushes, the silkiness of raffia or the rough flakiness of bark.

Mixing natural and unnatural fibres

Tʜᴇ industrial society of the twentieth century produced a new source of material – synthetic waste. Particularly in the Third World recycling has always been a way of life and these flexible, colourful, long-lasting materials were quickly incorporated into basketry. The contrasts that can be achieved by juxtaposing natural and man-made fibres are the most stunning of all as colour and texture are both thrown into relief by the inherent differences.

Aʙᴏᴠᴇ: *Nineteenth-century mat from the Aleutian Islands; it has been twined in a spiral, starting around a Nigerian coin. The foundation is of grass decorated with yarn and bird quills.*
Lᴇꜰᴛ: *Bundle-coiled grass basket from the Gambia. Both the handle and the spaced stitching have been worked using recycled, man-made packing tape.*
Bᴇʟᴏw: *'Cephalods I and II' – contemporary sculptural basketry made from willow and synthetic fibre by Mary Butcher, England.*
Oᴘᴘᴏsɪᴛᴇ, ᴀʙᴏᴠᴇ, ʟᴇꜰᴛ: *A group of fancy stake and strand baskets made by Mohawk Indians in New York State in around 1900 using ash splints for stakes and sweetgrass,* Hierochloe odorata *or* Savastana odorata, *for weavers.*
Oᴘᴘᴏsɪᴛᴇ, ᴀʙᴏᴠᴇ, ʀɪɢʜᴛ: *Large fan (length: 77 cm, 30¼ in.) from northeast India. The pattern has been achieved by twill plaiting using strips of bamboo along the fan and doubled strips of rattan across.*
Oᴘᴘᴏsɪᴛᴇ, ᴍᴀɪɴ ᴘɪᴄᴛᴜʀᴇ: *A pair of storage pots from the Indonesian island of Lombok. The main structure is of twill-plaited bamboo wrapped at intervals in palm leaf. The surface is rubbed with coconut oil to provide a sheen.*
Oᴘᴘᴏsɪᴛᴇ, ʙᴇʟᴏw, ʀɪɢʜᴛ: *Bowl, from Bangladesh, made of coiled palm fibre sewn with strips of silver foil.*

EMBROIDERY

THE act of applying decoration with fibres or threads to the surface of an otherwise completed basket can be easier and quicker than creating a pattern during the weaving process. Although in the USA during the nineteenth century it was fashionable to embroider with woollen yarn on baskets bought for the purpose, the practice has never been particularly common and frequently gives the impression of being an afterthought. Embroidery most often appears on goods that have been mass produced for export.

ABOVE: *Kuba basket, from the Democratic Republic of Congo, with French knots in raffia.*

Raffia embroidery

EMBROIDERY executed in raffia is the most frequently found form of embroidery on baskets. In China, floral designs stitched with brightly dyed raffia or synthetic imitations have been worked on sewing baskets made of plaited rice straw since the time of the British Empire and maybe before, and similar work is now produced on plaited rush boxes in the Philippines. Long stitches are used partly for speed, but also to display the silky lustre of the raffia fibres.

In the Kasai river region of Zaire (Democratic Republic of Congo) raffia cloth is produced as a prestige textile by the Kuba and has even been used as currency. Baskets are sometimes embroidered with raffia twisted into tight knots or worked like a shaggy mane.

Other fibres

ANY fibre that is fine or can be slit into strips can be used for sewing coils together or for surface embroidery. Palm leaves are ideal as they are so flexible. Grasses may also be employed, but are most suitable when working geometric designs with a limited number of bends.

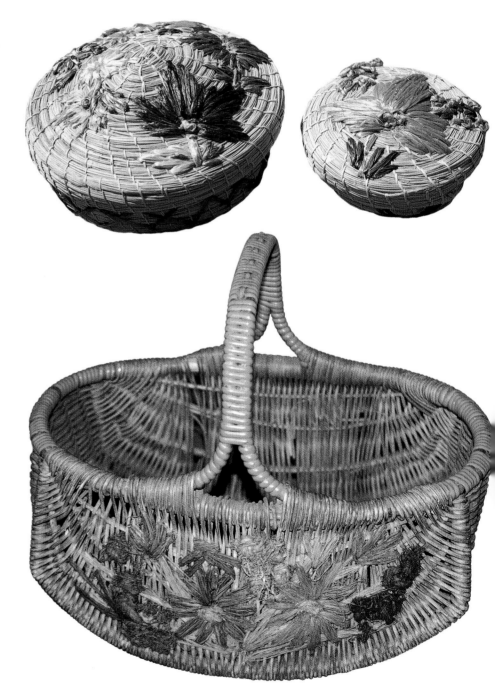

THREE

Slips and spills

An effect similar to embroidery can be created by using short splints which are held in place by tucking each end into the weave of a basket wall. This simple technique is used to create herringbone designs on the cheap, mass-produced Chinese baskets that are possibly the most common basket in the world. A far more sophisticated version is employed in the manufacture of Japanese flower-arranging containers. Finer patterns using thin spills are worked by the Kayan of Kalimantan in imitation of more complex twill-plaited designs.

OPPOSITE, CENTRE: *Cellophane embroidery on coiled grass pots.*
OPPOSITE, BELOW, LEFT: *Mexican sombrero with advertising crudely embroidered on it.*
OPPOSITE, BELOW, RIGHT: *Shopping basket with dyed raffia embroidery.*
ABOVE, LEFT: *One of the commonest baskets in the world is this type made for export in China. Here the surface has been decorated with spills slipped between the structural elements.*
ABOVE, RIGHT: *A Kayan plaited bag, from Kalimantan, decorated with short dyed spills tucked into the surface.*

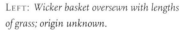

LEFT: *Wicker basket oversewn with lengths of grass; origin unknown.*
BELOW: *A Chinese plaited straw fan decorated with motifs built up with short, dyed straws.*

EMBELLISHMENT

Eᴍʙʀᴏɪᴅᴇʀʏ is rarely used to decorate the surface of baskets, but the attachment of all manner of small trinkets, trifles and natural objects to build up a decorative effect is widespread. Sometimes beads or other small items may be incorporated during the construction of a basket.

Function

Tʜᴇ purpose of embellishment is usually purely decorative, but certain colours and specific items may serve a talismanic or prophylactic function. Mirrors and blue beads, for instance, are commonly used on textiles, jewelry and baskets to avert the evil eye and to protect their owners from harm. However, nothing creates a more eye-catching sparkle than a piece of glass and so it is virtually impossible to separate the two functions entirely.

Beads

Bᴇᴀᴅs are one of the world's oldest trade items and their display has often been used as a show of wealth. Generally small and available in a wide range of colours, they are ideal in large quantities for building up colourful patterns, sometimes spiritual and often of great complexity.

Beads may be threaded on to the foundation material of a basket, sewn on afterwards or worked into a net which is attached to the basket after it has been constructed.

Beads can be made from many materials and many man-made objects, such as buttons or coins, may be used in the same way.

Shells

Tʜᴇ most widely used shell is the cowrie, *Cypraea moneta*, which was once used as a form of currency thousands of miles away from its place of origin

Tᴏᴘ: *Two Ethiopian coiled basketry pots. On the left, strings of glass beads have been sewn onto the finished basket, whereas on the right beads have been threaded onto the fibre used to stitch the coils.*
Aʙᴏᴠᴇ, ʟᴇғᴛ: *Coiled reed and palm-fibre bowl, from western Pakistan, with a mirror in the centre. Mirrors feature prominently in the embroidered textiles of the region.*
Aʙᴏᴠᴇ, ʀɪɢʜᴛ: *Bamboo pot, from Myanmar (Burma), coated with lacquer and encrusted with gold paint and coloured glass.*

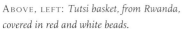

ABOVE, LEFT: *Tutsi basket, from Rwanda, covered in red and white beads.*

ABOVE, CENTRE: *Ethiopian coiled grass pot decorated with cowrie shells.*

ABOVE, RIGHT: *Chinese tiffin basket decorated with beads, coins and tassels.*

BELOW: *Feather-covered 'gift' or 'jewel' basket with abalone and clam shells, made by the Pomo of California.*

BOTTOM: *Four Chippewa birch bark baskets with porcupine-quill decoration, Great Lakes area, Canada.*

in the Indian Ocean. It is particularly prized as a fertility talisman because of its resemblance to female genitalia. Mother of pearl is also common, most often in the form of recycled buttons.

Other natural objects

THE quills of birds' feathers were used by the indigenous peoples of the Aleutian Islands in their coiled baskets to incorporate a subtle sheen, but even more scintillating effects are still achieved by the Pomos of California who use the brightly coloured plumage of a number of birds in their 'gift' baskets.

Porcupine quills are a common decorative feature of sweetgrass or birch bark baskets made in the woodlands of the northeastern USA and Canada.

The range of objects used for embellishment is vast, restricted only by local availability and the imagination of the basketmaker.

FAR LEFT: *Bowls from around the world.*
TOP LEFT: *Zulu grain pot.*
TOP CENTRE: *Child's lunch box, Madeira.*
TOP RIGHT: *Lacquered sheath, northern Thailand.*

FROM THE CRADLE TO THE GRAVE

ABOVE, CENTRE: *Bowl for winnowing chaff; bought in England.*
NEAR LEFT: *Mats from Thailand.*

EVERYDAY BASKETRY

LEFT: *Washing an elephant with a bailer plaited from split bamboo, Mae Sa in northern Thailand.*
RIGHT: *Plaited sifters and winnowing trays are used all over the world. This selection includes examples from China, Japan, Thailand and England. Archaeological finds have suggested that the yucca ring sifters still used by the Pueblo peoples of New Mexico and Arizona in the USA have remained unchanged since about 2000 BC.*

BASKETMAKERS are able to produce an incredible variety of containers and utensils, using whatever materials are available, a little muscle and a range of skills. Their knowledge and adaptability have been applied so well to virtually all walks of life that baskets are now taken for granted. They are light, easy to carry, more durable than ceramics and will stand a considerable amount of stress. Furthermore, the process of making a basket has, on the whole, been considerably easier than making and firing a ceramic pot or forging a metal one and even though in modern times it may only cost a small amount to purchase a plastic container, in the developing world basketmaking skills may be available, but not a supply of cash.

FOUR

BELOW: *'Flour' basket, from Shanxi province, belonging to a Chinese farmer's wife.*
RIGHT: *Kayan longhouse in Borneo; photographed in 1892. Fish traps and mats are stacked against the wall.*

LEFT: *Ifugao* takba, *a back pack used by hunters in the hills of the northern Philippines.*
RIGHT: *Armenian fruit pedlars in Bitlis, Kurdistan.*
RIGHT, CENTRE: *Baskets used to cover the indigo dye pits at Kano, Nigeria.*
BELOW, LEFT: *Baskets for sale a hundred years ago at an agricultural hardware store in Greece.*
BELOW, RIGHT: *A Thai woman resting after carrying fruit and vegetables to the market at Petchaburi.*

In the 'developed' world many of the functions once fulfilled by baskets have been taken over by mass-produced plastic and metal objects, but in the developing world the hardware store or market is still stocked high with basketry for every task. Even in the West where industrialization exerts a stranglehold many of us still prefer a 'natural' basket and there must be precious few who live in a home completely devoid of basketry – maybe a linen basket, log basket, bicycle basket, sewing basket or waste-paper basket.

123

FROM THE CRADLE...

For millennia baskets have been an indispensable part of our daily lives and many of us spend our first days lying in a cradle. The very word 'cradle' is derived from the Latin *cratis*, meaning a basket made of wickerwork. It is only too fitting that the Worshipful Company of Basketmakers chose 'a cradle, therein a child, rocked at the head by a girl and at the feet by a boy, both vested, all proper' for the crest of their coat of arms.

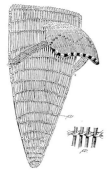

Top: Hupa cradle, California

Above: Ute cradle, Utah

Above: *Pharaoh's daughter finding Moses in the bulrushes.*

Distribution

In the Bible (Exodus 2, iii) we are told that the basket in which Moses was set afloat was made of rushes or papyrus and coated with slime or pitch. In England the wicker 'Moses basket' is still a popular babies' cot – it is light, well ventilated and homely. Early perambulators were also made with a wicker structure which is imitated in plastic dolls' prams today.

The Native American papoose was swaddled and fastened to a cradle board which could be carried on the mother's back or set down safely in a convenient place. These were sometimes made of solid wood, but were often of a wicker construction. An arched section might be included so that a hood could be attached to keep the infant's head out of the sun. Cradleboards are not in common usage anymore, but they are still made, often in miniature, for sale as souvenirs.

Above: *Yuma wicker cradle covered in cloth, California, USA.*
Below: *Baby carrier from Kalimantan. This was originally covered with a colourful beaded net.*
Bottom: *Imbricated spruce-root cradle from the Thompson River in British Columbia, Canada.*

RIGHT: *A Dani woman's* bilum *of interlooped cotton and wild orchid fibre from Irian Jaya, Indonesia.*
INSET: *Baby cradled in a* bilum, *Port Moresby, Papua New Guinea.*
BELOW, LEFT: *A fitched willow rocking cradle from the Channel Island of Guernsey.*
BELOW, RIGHT: *Dutch baby restraint made from coiled straw by Ian Beaty.*

The interlooped *bilum* of New Guinea is soft and capacious. It is used to carry produce, pigs, shopping or babies and can be readily hung up with a sleeping baby inside.

In many parts of the world some common form of basket is adapted – in terms of its size and shape and perhaps the addition of handles by which it may be hung up – for use as a cradle.

Toddlers

THE Dutch had a novel solution to the problem of curious toddlers getting into trouble. They placed the child into the top of a cylindrical container made of coiled straw from where it could see what was going on, but not get underfoot.

For his home at Kettles Yard, the Cambridge art collector Jim Ede is reputed to have kept his offspring away from his precious objets d'art by imprisoning them in large, specially commissioned play pens based on traditional lobster pots.

COAT OF ARMS OF
THE WORSHIPFUL
COMPANY OF
BASKETMAKERS

FOUR

WHEN carrying a burden on the head or on a pole at least one hand must be free and so it is not a practicable method of transporting goods across steep, or uneven terrain, or through thick vegetation where the hands are constantly needed in case of stumbling and the body is leaning forwards. It is, however, widespread on plains and level ground.

The ancient origins of this method of transportation are verified by Ancient Egyptian hieroglyphs where the verb 'to carry' was represented by a pictogram of a man with a basket on his head. Pre-dating the hieroglyphs are Sumerian stone reliefs from about 3000 BC which show the Babylonian priest-king Ur-Nină carrying a basket of building materials on his head at the founding of the temple of Ningirsu in Lagash.

On the head

WIDE, shallow baskets with a low centre of gravity are most suitable for carrying on the head. With good posture it is possible to carry surprisingly heavy loads as the weight is spread straight down the spine. For short distances virtually anything can be carried in this way with support from the hands. Skilful porters at London's old Covent Garden

ABOVE: *Nuns in Myanmar (Burma) collecting alms in baskets carried on their heads.*
LEFT: *Fruit baskets used by the Chivers jam company in Cambridgeshire, England.*
LEFT, INSET: *A porter at the old Covent Garden Market in London, England.*
BELOW: *Portuguese women once carried everything, including their children, on their heads.*
OPPOSITE, TOP: *Shallow twined baskets, from Zimbabwe, ideal for carrying on the head.*

market took pride in being able to carry baskets of fruit and vegetables stacked twenty high on their heads!

On a pole

CARRYING loads suspended from either end of a stout pole balanced on one shoulder, rather like a pair of scales, is another widespread practice. The shape of the baskets is not particularly important as long as the weight can be distributed evenly between front and back. Often, as in Thailand, a shallow basket is used with an exaggerated handle or frame from which it can be hung.

In Europe, a yoke, carved to fit comfortably around the neck, has been used for centuries to carry market baskets, harvest baskets, or milk pails with the weight spread across both shoulders, reducing the strain on the arms and hands.

FOUR

ABOVE: *Thai frames for suspending baskets from a pole.*
LEFT: *Japanese trader carrying produce on a pole.*
RIGHT: *Dutch woman with yoke and baskets.*
BELOW: *A wooden yoke from Guernsey.*

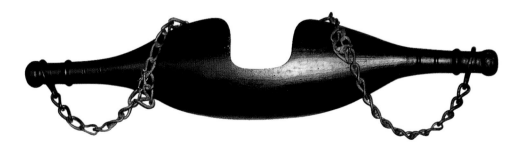

CARRYING ON THE BACK

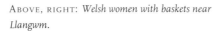

WHEN walking in the hills, over uneven terrain, or along tracks obscured by vegetation, it is necessary to keep one's hands free in the event of stumbling. Highland and hill-tribe burden baskets are therefore carried on the back. In the interests of stability, their height exceeds their width and they are frequently conical, tapering in towards the base. Some are small, while others, like those once used in the mountains of Italy, extend from the top of the head to the knees.

The type of weave varies according to the intended contents, for example, they are densely woven for grain, but have an open weave for firewood or animal fodder. Many are shaped to fit into the curves of the back.

To prevent spilling the load while the bearer struggles out of the straps, burden baskets are sometimes fitted with flat bases or feet.

Tump-lines

A TUMP-LINE is a strap that passes across the forehead to take the weight of the load off the back. The section that rests on the forehead is broad or padded for comfort. The other end passes under the bottom of the basket or through loops near the base. The word 'tump' is Native American in origin, but baskets are also carried in this way in many distant regions such as Nepal. A strap of this kind is manufactured separately from the basket and may be of a totally different material.

FOUR

Shoulder straps

SHOULDER straps are the most widely used way of supporting a back pack. They need to be wide enough on the

ABOVE, RIGHT: *Welsh women with baskets near Llangwm.*

BELOW, LEFT: *Collecting seaweed on the Isle of Skye.*

BELOW, RIGHT: *Yekuana burden basket, from the Amazon jungle, decorated with armadillo motifs.*

shoulder so that they don't dig in, but otherwise can be quite narrow. They are normally made separately and then attached securely to the basket.

More flexible than burden baskets, duffel bags and knapsacks are carried in this way. A fine example is the Penan *ambong* from Sarawak which is used to carry personal belongings when travelling. These are soft and light and boldly decorated.

Chest straps

A STRAP can be stretched across the chest to carry a basket. This method means the bearer has to lean forward from the waist and take much of the weight on their hips and legs.

ABOVE, LEFT: *Macusi reed burden basket, from Guyana, in four-strand plaiting.*

TOP CENTRE: *Hex-weave bamboo burden basket from Nepal.*

TOP RIGHT: *Vietnamese woman, from the Mien Trung region, with back pack during French colonial times, early twentieth century.*

CENTRE: *Hmong burden baskets for sale at Doi Pui, a hill village in northern Thailand (450 baht is about £7).*

RIGHT: *Hill-tribe burden baskets, from Thailand (left) and, on the right, an Akha basket from Myanmar (Burma).*

CARRYING IN THE HAND

A BASKET small enough to be carried in the hand or with an arm through the handle is an indispensable utensil, particularly for women, the world over. Most frequently employed for carrying produce to and from the market or shops, they are often referred to simply as 'shopping' baskets or 'arm' baskets. At many times in history, in a variety of forms, small baskets with handles have become fashion accessories, and used as handbags.

Baskets of this type are not intended to be used for carrying heavy items any distance as the weight is concentrated in the handle which can dig into the hand. There are two main types – the rigid basket with a single handle and the soft basket with two.

Rigid baskets

WHETHER of willow, bamboo or rattan, round or elliptical, baskets with a single stout handle spanning the middle are to be found all over the world. Most are stake and strand, but in forested regions such as Finland or the Appalachian Mountains of North America they can be of plaited bark or split wood.

ABOVE: *A distinctive form of basket common in Shanxi province, northern China.*
LEFT: *Plaited birch bark basket made by Santeri Jekkonen, a Finnish basketmaker.*
BELOW: *A fashionable young woman, from Martinique, equipped with a basketry handbag.*

Frame baskets such as the English Southport basket belong to this group, as does the 'hen' basket. Known in Scotland as an 'ose' and in Germany as a 'rocking boat' basket, they are constructed with a framework made from a set of hoops of diminishing size which meet at the handle. They are so strong that in medieval Europe they were used for hoisting building materials up scaffolding.

Soft baskets

Soft baskets can be constructed by plaiting, twining, looping or coiling using pliable materials such as palm leaves, rushes or grasses. They are stiff enough to retain their shape, but flexible enough to accommodate many inconsistent shapes.

A loop handle is attached to each side and the bag is carried with both handles gripped in one hand. They are generally rectangular rather than round. The modern plastic bag is a contemporary version of this type of basket.

FOUR

ABOVE: *Wrapped coil palm baskets, from India, with handles sewn on.*
BELOW, LEFT: *Zulu* isikhwama *twill plaited from ilala palm in South Africa.*
BELOW, RIGHT: *Plaited palm bags, from Sri Lanka, with patterns created by the colour placement method.*

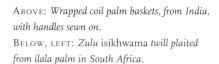

TOP: *'Hen' baskets such as this one are believed to have been in use in Scotland in Celtic times, but are now common all across Europe. This one was bought in Yugoslavia thirty years ago.*
ABOVE: *An* Arundo donax *basket, from the Greek island of Lemnos, of a type found all around the Aegean.*

BEASTS OF BURDEN

Ever since man first domesticated animals he has needed the means to bend them to his will and exploit their strength. Subsequently, having taken on the responsibility of their welfare, he has had to develop equipment to help him care for them. Whatever the animal – horse, camel, donkey or llama – the problem of controlling and caring for them has been solved in similar ways.

Tackle

The harness and bridle used to keep an animal under control must be tough and flexible and are most often made of strips or braids of leather, but occasionally basketry techniques have been used to stunning effect. The Native Americans of the American Plains, Plateau and Basin produced intricate gear of natural or brightly dyed horsehair coiled around a central core of rawhide.

Panniers

For stability, animal burdens most often consist of a pair of bags or baskets which are slung over the animal, with one on either side and are known as panniers. Although any multi-purpose basket may be employed, sometimes a specific shape or size is required because of the contents or the animal. One distinctive example is the flat-sided shell-fish pannier used well into the twentieth century on donkeys and ponies by English fishermen on the Suffolk coast.

RIGHT: *A quirt, or horsewhip, made by Utes from Utah, USA, by coiling and stitching horsehair around a rawhide core.*
BELOW: *Camels at a Tunisian waterhole; their humps are covered with matting.*

Animal husbandry

Dealing with livestock often requires restraining them or at least ensuring protection from their teeth. Muzzles may be quite sophisticated or consist of a simply twisted strand of fibre, while for greater restraint, for medical purposes or to transport an animal to market, larger basketry tubes or cylinders have also been developed in many places to fit around a beast's neck or whole body.

Roman basketmakers were sometimes called upon to make *solea spartea* to protect the feet of cattle and horses, a craft that continued in Japan where pack animals were, in living memory, still fitted with

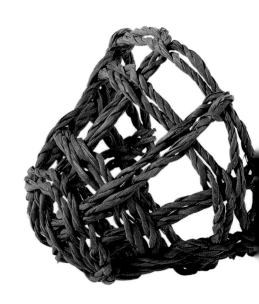

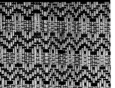

shoes made from rice straw to protect them from sharp stones.

Bicycles

During the twentieth century the bicycle took on many of the functions of beasts of burden as it was used both for personal transport and as a delivery vehicle. Baskets were developed to fit over the front wheel, which was often smaller than the rear wheel to accommodate a large basket, and panniers to fit over the rear wheel.

ENGLISH WOMAN GOING TO MARKET, AFTER A SEVENTEENTH-CENTURY WOODBLOCK PRINT

OPPOSITE, BELOW, LEFT: *A French girl, in Normandy, leading her donkey loaded with wicker panniers.*

OPPOSITE, BELOW, RIGHT: *A Japanese ox muzzle constructed by ply splitting, a process in which fibres are threaded through openings where the ply has been twisted open.*

RIGHT: *An English student transporting books and provisions in a basket on her bicycle; a mechanical beast of burden.*

ABOVE, LEFT: *Rattan pannier used by English fishermen in Suffolk to transport their catch on pony or donkey back.*

TOP RIGHT: *Carrying goods in coiled plait panniers at Dendera, Egypt.*

ABOVE: *A collar once used in England to immobilize cows during veterinary procedures.*

BUYING AND SELLING

SINCE ancient times whenever people from different communities or professions have come together to trade and barter baskets have played an important part in the process. Traders and shoppers, market stalls and supermarkets all rely on baskets.

AZTEC MARKET, AFTER A DRAWING FROM THE SIXTEENTH-CENTURY *CODEX MENDOZA*

FAR LEFT: *Fruit and vegetables for sale at Sweta market, Lombok.*
ABOVE: *Weighing produce in Algeria using coiled plait baskets.*
BELOW: *Potatoes for sale at St Peter Port market, Guernsey.*

The trader

A trader must wrap and carry his or her merchandise safely to market or to the shop. Often this requires containers specially prepared for the task which may be thrown away afterwards. Many of the baskets seen at a Polynesian market, for instance, have been made as needed from a palm leaf and will be used only once. Others may be sturdy and can be used time and time again.

Today, customers are often offered a wire basket or trolley to carry their purchases until they are packed into plastic bags when they pay.

Display

ON a stall or shop shelves produce is often displayed in shallow baskets or trays that keep the different items separate, but still allow a clear view. Particularly common are the large round plaited trays, resembling those used for winnowing, that can be seen in markets from Turkey to the Philippines.

FOUR

Packaging

Putting produce into handy packs is not a recent invention. In Roman times cheese was packed into a special basket woven from rushes called a *fiscella*, the predecessor of the plastic tub. In modern convenience food outlets portions are dispensed in polystyrene trays, but in Thailand where fast food is often two small fish the disposable container would probably still be a crudely woven basket tray.

The shopper

The shopper has always availed himself or herself of a sturdy and capacious bag or basket that is easy to carry and is light when empty. A particularly common type in the West is the round or elliptical wicker shopping basket with a rope handle.

Until late in the twentieth century in Western Europe a wheeled basket with a long handle was often used. This made it possible to buy a larger quantity than could physically be carried.

Above, left: *A fish stall at Petchaburi market, Thailand. Large trays are used to display the fish and small baskets for take-away packaging.*
Above, right: *Two versions of English willow 'boat' baskets. Both are frame baskets with an attached handle.*
Right: *A shopping basket made from centre cane and buff willow; decorated with plastic strips.*
Below: *Twined market baskets made in Ghana from dyed savannah grass. Similar baskets are made in Kenya from twined sisal and have leather straps.*

Opposite, bottom: *Packaging. Left: Thai bamboo baskets for portions of fish. Centre: French veneer box for Camembert cheese. Right: French willow containers for Neuchâtel cheese.*

135

PROTECTION

Whaen transporting fragile materials such as ceramics, glass and gourds or even vegetables the number of breakages can be greatly reduced by packing or wrapping in a basketry shell.

Crates

Crates used to transport goods were originally wicker hampers or baskets. Like 'cradle', the word 'crate' is derived from the Latin cratis, meaning a wicker basket. These days many crates are made of nailed wooden slats or interwoven wire, but as they are generally made as cheaply as possible at the place of manufacture or shipping they are still sometimes constructed from bamboo, rattan or any local material. They are made large enough so they can be lined with straw or paper to cushion their contents. Their construction is tough, but crude, as a crate is often dumped after a single use.

Fitted containers

Individual items such as jars or wine carboys, which are of a standard size, may be placed in a purpose-made basket that fits tightly.

Decorative covers for bottles are sometimes made with such care that they become more valuable than their contents.

ABOVE: *Basket for transporting large pottery; from Morocco.*

ABOVE, RIGHT: *English stoneware jugs in wicker covers.*

RIGHT: *Spanish or Portuguese glass wine, or oil, bottle encased in skeined willow.*

BELOW, LEFT: *Twined grass bottle covers, from Ghana; similar to those made by the Makah of Washington State, USA.*

BELOW, RIGHT: *Reuseable twined rush bottle cover from Luzon in the Philippines.*

'TRAVELLING BOTTLE' FROM THE 1927/28 CATALOGUE OF HALL & ANDERSON, CALCUTTA, INDIA

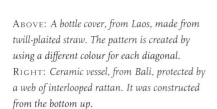

ABOVE: *A bottle cover, from Laos, made from twill-plaited straw. The pattern is created by using a different colour for each diagonal.*
RIGHT: *Ceramic vessel, from Bali, protected by a web of interlooped rattan. It was constructed from the bottom up.*
BELOW, LEFT: *A gourd in a hex-weave casing used to carry liquids by the Akha people of the Chiang Rai area in the far north of Thailand.*
BELOW, RIGHT: *Lacquered rice pot protected by interlaced rattan strips; made in the Chiang Mai area of northern Thailand.*

For this reason they may have a detachable section so that the bottle can be changed. This style of basketry has usually been adapted from traditional techniques in order to make items intended for sale rather than home use.

A second skin

CONSUMMATE skill is needed to construct a layer which fits exactly around the contours of a bottle or gourd. Water is the most vital of all commodities and great care is often taken to make sure that a container does not get damaged and its contents lost, so in Asia, Africa and the Americas gourds, in particular, have been wrapped with fibres interlinked in many different ways. Despite the simple beauty of much of this work, once the container itself is broken the basketry is of no use and is thrown away.

FOUR

FISHING

The practice of fishing in fresh or salt water has been a matter of survival for communities all round the globe and a source of recreation for those who can afford leisure time. The need to trap and store fish, anywhere from Norfolk to Nagasaki, from New Zealand to Newfoundland, has spawned an enormous number of ingenious solutions. All baskets made for fishing are woven loosely enough to allow water to run out, but tightly enough to retain the captured fish.

Active traps

In shallow waters, such as flooded padi fields, fishermen may equip themselves with a simple conical basket with an open weave. Both ends are left open so that, on spotting a fish, the fisherman can stab the device down and then put his hand in through the top to remove his prey.

LEFT: *A Norfolk eel trap made from white willow and cane by Terry Bensley. (Length 90 cm, 35 in.)*
BELOW: *Cambodian fish trap of rattan and wood. This is an active trap used in shallow water.*

Another technique, often used by a team of fishermen or even a whole village, is to wade through water driving any fish into a restricted space where they are scooped up in loosely woven baskets.

Passive traps

Other types of trap can be placed in a likely spot and left. One end is fitted with a narrow tapering opening through which fish can squeeze, attracted by bait left inside. Once in the trap the captured fish is unable to get back out. The design of this type of trap varies according to the size of the intended victim – large and capacious for lobsters, but long and narrow for eels.

Storage

Line fishermen often use live bait which must be kept fresh. Fishermen in Guernsey still employ a distinctive elliptical basket, called a *courge*, although now metal and plastic have replaced the traditional willow. This is filled with live sand eels and trailed in the water behind the boats.

When fishing from a boat with a net, the catch may be left loose in the bottom of the boat until the return to shore when it is unloaded in baskets. These are sometimes made to hold a specific volume of fish. For example, the cran, used to hold herrings, was stamped by an official to show it was the correct size.

The individual fisherman using a line, traps or small hand net usually carries a creel at his hip into which fish are dropped through a small hole in the top.

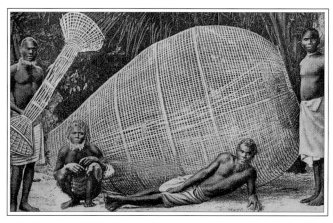

FOUR

Top: *Willow 'grig' for trapping eels, once common in the English fens.*
Above, middle left: *A small Norfolk herring cran made by Colin Manthorpe.*
Above, middle right: *Giant deep-sea fish trap from New Britain, Papua New Guinea.*
Right: *Fish creel worn at the hip by fishermen from Lombok, Indonesia.*

BIRDS

BIRDS have been a source of food and entertainment since time immemorial. The transition from hunting to domesticating birds necessitated the development of cages and containers that would keep a bird captive, but also allow the passage of light and air.

Food

SOME fowl intended for the table are kept permanently cooped up, but most are allowed to wander about scavenging for food. They may be held in a compound, restrained on a leash or have their primary feathers clipped, but at night they may be caged and hung out of the reach of prowling predators.

Carrying fowl to market to sell them also requires a basket, often made to contain a number of birds. In the West these are generally wicker, but in the East they most often have a hexagonal plaited structure of bamboo or rattan.

Nests

TO encourage the breeding of captive and wild birds artificial nests were once common in Western Europe. They

OPPOSITE, TOP: *A Dutch man-made duck's nest.*

OPPOSITE, CENTRE: *English wicker duck's nest.*

OPPOSITE, BOTTOM LEFT: *An English bird carrier made from skeined willow.*

OPPOSITE, BOTTOM RIGHT: *English copy of a Dutch chicken basket.*

ABOVE: *Basket for fighting cocks, Xishuang Banna, Yunnan, China.*

RIGHT: *A pair of wooden cages for song birds; made in Lombok, Indonesia.*

INSET: *Cage, from southern Thailand, used to hold a barred ground dove bred competitively because of its song.*

also provided a source of freshly laid eggs. More recently, environmental concerns have led to the use of artificial nests to encourage the breeding of rare and endangered species.

Pigeons

THE breeding of pigeons for racing has been a popular pastime in areas such as the north of England for centuries. Special baskets like hampers are used to transport the birds to distant locations where, upon release, they set off for home as fast as they can.

Homing pigeons were also once widely used to carry messages, often of a military or secret nature. They, too, were carried in a basket.

Fighting cocks

ALTHOUGH the 'sport' of cock fighting is now illegal in much of the West, it still thrives in Asia. Breeders keep their prize specimens isolated so that they cannot disembowel each other with their vicious spurs.

Songs and plumage

THE most elegant bird baskets are the cages built for birds who delight their owners with their melodious songs or colourful plumage. Wire is now commonly used, but the most expensive cages are still made from bamboo in Thailand.

SHEATHS AND SCABBARDS

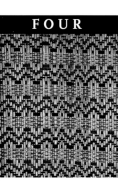

THE most vital piece of equipment for a man working in the field, forest or jungle is a good knife. It hangs at his side or on his back, where it is never out of reach, in a stout sheath that will prevent him injuring himself and will also keep the blade safe from damage. Whereas a herdsman might use a leather sheath, a forest dweller generally opts for one of wood or plant fibre.

Basket sheaths

THE *hobuk* is a *dao* sheath used in Arunachal Pradesh which is made by folding in half a mat made of rattan or bamboo splints sewn together along the side and bottom. A more elaborate version is made in the Philippines by the Bagobo who decorate theirs with hair and carved wooden edging.

The hill tribes of Laos, Myanmar (Burma) and northern Thailand (the Golden Triangle) make very tough sheaths and quivers by folding bamboo strips in half and weaving around the ends to form a conical mouth.

The epitome of Japanese skill is perhaps the beautiful fittings made for Samurai swords, complete with elaborate lacings on the hilt, but humble woodcutters contented themselves with sheaths for their hatchets plaited from split oak bark.

Beautiful two-tone twill-plaited quivers are sometimes made by the Makú of the Amazon rain forest to hold the darts for their blow pipes.

In Bali basketmakers make themselves impromptu sheaths for their knives. These *saung* are made by skilfully folding the two halves of a palm leaflet which are still partly connected along the spine.

ABOVE, LEFT: *Palm-leaf knife sheath copied from a* saung *made by a Balinese basketmaker in just a few minutes.*
ABOVE: *Malay toddy tapper; the tools of his trade are in a container strapped to his side.*
BELOW, LEFT: *A sheath of plaited split bamboo used by the Kamu of Laos.*

ABOVE: *A mizunara bark hatchet sheath used until the 1930s by woodcutters in the Ina district of Nagano prefecture, Japan.*
BELOW: *Iban men from Sarawak armed with large knives in wooden sheaths bound with bands of basketry.*

Wooden sheaths

SIMPLE quivers are made by the Apa Tani of Arunachal Pradesh in northeast India from a bamboo tube closed at the bottom by the node. The top is fitted with a lid of woven cane.

A common style of sheath is typified by the type found in Nagaland, northeast India. The knife, *dao*, is carried in a sheath made from two slightly hollowed slats of wood bound together with plaited cane. In

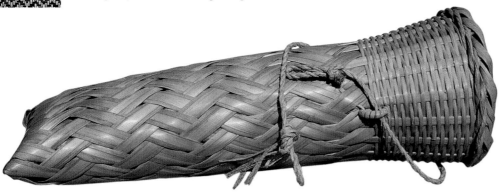

ABOVE: Bolo *and sheath from the Banue area in the Philippines.*
BELOW, LEFT: *Akha bamboo sheath from Myanmar (Burma). Centre: Kamu bamboo sheath from Laos.*
BELOW, RIGHT: *Akha rattan sheath from northern Thailand.*

the Philippines sheaths for a *bolo* made in this way may be completely covered in woven rattan.

Another technique is to carve a hollow on one face of a single piece of wood and hold the blade in with plaited bands. This style is favoured by the Ifugao in the north of the Philippines and the Akha of Thailand and Myanmar (Burma). The latter attach a tubular basket to the front of the sheath for carrying other equipment or collected items.

143

GATHERING

The earliest humans survived by hunting and gathering. They collected what they could find and moved on. In a few remote corners of the globe this way of life continues virtually unchanged, giving us a glimpse into the lifestyle of our ancestors. Tools and utensils are limited to perhaps only a knife, a spear, a digging stick and a few baskets.

The simplest piece of basketry used for gathering is probably a mat. Easily rolled up, it could be used for catching fruit, seeds or nuts when laid under a tree or bush, or for carrying foodstuff, or for drying it in the sun, or as a surface for sorting and preparing. One example is the *isithebe* used by the Zulus. Often decorated with subtle twilled patterns, these indispensable articles are made from twined *imizi* rushes.

PAIUTE SEED BEATER,
AFTER A DRAWING
REPRODUCED IN
INDIAN BASKETRY
BY GEORGE
WHARTON JAMES

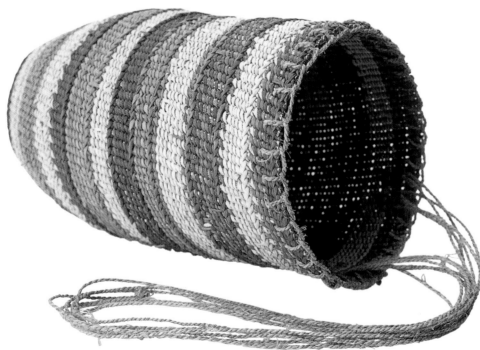

General purpose bags

STRETCHY or collapsible bags such as the *bilum* of New Guinea or the dilly bag used by Australian aborigines were once the stock in trade of opportunist hunter-gatherers. However, they were also adept at constructing instant baskets and containers out of any materials to hand and were therefore able to travel very light and move fast.

Seeds

THE gathering of the seeds of wild grasses for grinding into meal began in prehistoric times. Native Americans of California and the American Southwest continued harvesting wild grains on a regular basis into the early twentieth century. The seeds were knocked into a basket with a seed beater or harvesting wand of interlaced twigs bound with yucca fibre.

Nuts and fruits

To harvest nuts or fruits demands either shaking or hitting the tree or bush, or plucking them by hand, one at

a time. Baskets of different shapes and sizes are employed according to the softness of the fruit.

The nature of a community's staple food has always dictated the shape of its baskets. For instance, acorns were the staple food of many indigenous Californians such as the Chumash and a variety of bowl-shaped baskets were developed specifically for all aspects of gathering, cleaning, preparing and cooking acorns. Further north on the northwest coast a large number of cylindrical baskets were made for gathering berries.

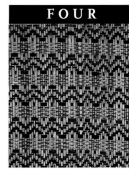

Above: *Tea pickers in the hills near Kazirangha, Assam, India.*
Opposite, top: *Nineteenth-century English willow basket used to collect eggs.*
Opposite, centre: *A willow basket employed when gathering nuts, made near Side, near Antalya in Turkey.*
Opposite, bottom: *Twined pandanus-fibre dilly bag made in four days by Elizabeth Mipilangurr from Arnhem Land in Australia's Northern Territories.*

Top left: *Zulu* isithebe, *a twined grass mat used for collecting food, made by the Hlubi sub-tribe.*
Above, centre: *Turkish willow basket for carrying peaches.*

Top right: *Willow basket used when picking apples; made in Eastern Europe to a British pattern.*
Above: *Coiled reed and palm basket for collecting food; made in Nigeria.*

145

AGRICULTURE

The transition to the active cultivation of crops led to the manufacture of a greater number of baskets for more specific tasks. Archetypal forms were developed, dictated by a combination of function and the materials available, and many have remained virtually unchanged for millennia. The yucca ring sifters used today by the Pueblo Indians of the American Southwest are identical to ones discovered by archaeologists dating back to 2000 BC.

Sowing and planting

Once the ground has been prepared, the commonest practice is to walk up and down the rows sowing or broadcasting seed from a basket slung at the waist. In Borneo the rice seed is treated with veneration and the baskets are often beautifully decorated. A crop such as potatoes, of course, demands the use of a larger, heavier basket placed on the ground.

Reaping and harvesting

The quantity harvested should be greater than the amount sown and so reaping demands larger baskets. Baskets used by a team are larger than those carried by an individual and those used to carry the crop home will be largest of all.

ABOVE: *A sculpture at the Royal Botanic Gardens at Kew, Surrey, England, showing a sower broadcasting seed from a seed lip.*
LEFT: *Iban basket, from Sarawak, used when sowing rice.*
BELOW, LEFT: *Kantu rice-harvesting basket from Kalimantan.*
BELOW, RIGHT: *Iban rice-harvesting basket from Sarawak.*
OPPOSITE, TOP LEFT: *Welsh willow* cyntell *used for harvesting potatoes; made by D. J. Davies.*
OPPOSITE, TOP RIGHT: *Hopi sifter from Arizona.*
OPPOSITE, CENTRE LEFT: *Twined seed basket from Gambella, Ethiopia.*
OPPOSITE, CENTRE RIGHT: *Threshing rice in Vietnam in the early twentieth century.*
OPPOSITE, BOTTOM: *Plaited winnowing tray from Vanuatu in the western Pacific.*

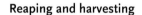

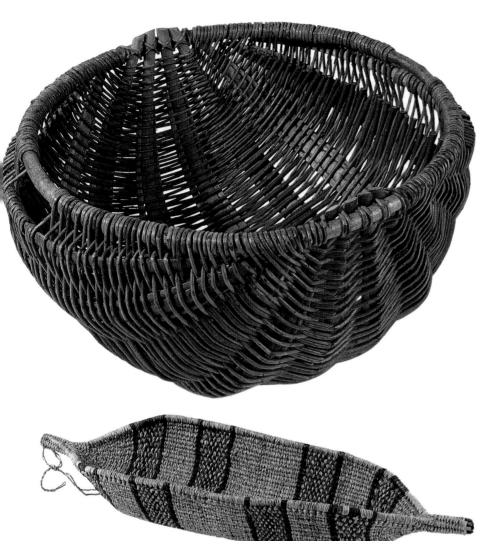

Sieving and sifting

A BASKET of harvested produce, particularly grains or beans, will probably contain many impurities such as stones, mud or insects. These must be removed by hand or by shaking the produce through a sieve or riddle. Sieves of different sizes may be employed for further sorting.

Threshing and winnowing

G RAIN is separated from stalks and husks by threshing. This may involve beating the grain with a hinged flail or crushing it under the hooves of oxen. The resulting mixture is then tossed into the air, sometimes with a shovel, but more often with a winnowing tray (circular) or a fan (open on one side), so that the wind can blow away the unwanted chaff while the heavier grains fall to the ground.

Finally, the crop will be stored for future use, frequently in a basketry structure of very large proportions.

FOUR

FENCES

At night time, in the same way their ancestors must have done, Masai herdsmen build a temporary barricade out of thorny branches to protect their precious cattle from attacks by lions. All around the world fences are built either to keep animals, or people, in or to keep them out.

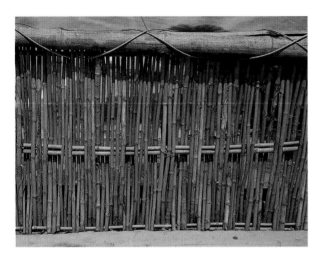

Bamboo fences

Bamboo is an ideal fence-building material. Easily collected anywhere from India to the Far East, whole culms make sturdy posts and thinner lengths or split cane are easily interlaced to form a barrier.

Hurdles

The wattle hurdle is a rectangular panel, about two metres (6^1⁄$_2$ ft) long, woven from hazel. They were once widely used by shepherds in Britain and Europe to make temporary enclosures for their sheep. Each hurdle was woven with a hole left in

Above: *The use of wattle hurdles in this show garden at the 1999 East of England Show demonstrates the continuing popularity of traditional materials among British gardeners.*
Left: *One style of bamboo fence frequently encountered in southern Thailand.*
Below, left: *Close up of a wattle fence in Cambridgeshire. To prevent splitting, the hazel rods must be twisted as they are bent around the end post.*

the centre. The shepherd could push a stick through the hole and so carry a number on his back to wherever they were needed.

Living fences

In Britain in the eighteenth and nineteenth centuries the Enclosure Acts enforced the hedging of fields. One of a farm labourer's tasks during the winter months was the 'laying' of these hedges to make sure that animals could not force their way through. This was accomplished by partly severing the stems (most often of hawthorn or blackthorn), bending them over and interlacing them around stakes driven into the ground at intervals. The resulting barrier was alive and impenetrable.

The planting of hedges, arches or even tunnels of interlaced willow rods is now fashionable in the West. They are so full of life that they easily root and burst into leaf.

Japanese fences

JAPANESE fencing has developed into an artistic range of styles for use in the garden. Bamboo is most common, but is often combined with other materials – with, for instance, bundles of withies to make a distinctive 'tea whisk' fence resembling a row of brushes standing upright.

Wire

MANY fences and enclosures are now constructed using prefabricated chicken wire or chain link, both of which are made of interlinked wire.

FIFTEENTH-
CENTURY
EUROPEAN
NATIVITY
SCENE
SHOWING
THE STABLE
ENCLOSED BY
HURDLES

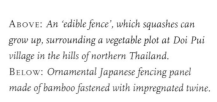

FOUR

ABOVE: *An 'edible fence', which squashes can grow up, surrounding a vegetable plot at Doi Pui village in the hills of northern Thailand.*
BELOW: *Ornamental Japanese fencing panel made of bamboo fastened with impregnated twine.*

ABOVE, LEFT: *Chestnut paling can be rolled up and moved as required. The split chestnut is held together by twined wire.*
ABOVE: *A living willow barrier planted at the University of Cambridge Botanical Gardens, England.*
LEFT: *A newly laid hedge in East Anglia, England. As a result of the Enclosure Acts in the eighteenth century there were once 600,000 miles of hedges in Britain.*

IN THE GARDEN

ARDENING, whether of essential food or decorative flowers, requires the use of barriers, tools and receptacles, much of which can be supplied by the application of basketmaking skills. The equipment required for vegetable culture needs to be robust, but when flowers are grown the emphasis is often on charm as well as practicality.

Collecting and carrying

For collecting vegetables from the garden or allotment smaller versions of agricultural baskets are ideal, but flowers require special treatment. To protect stems it is necessary to lay cut flowers flat and so baskets for flowers are most often long and flat. Many are circular in form with the sides bent up and drawn together by a handle.

Frames

Sweet peas, runner beans and other climbing plants require support. In the late twentieth century Western gardens saw a resurgence in the use of conical openwork 'wigwams' of hazel and willow not only as plant supports, but also as a decorative feature in their own right. In the East vegetables such as squashes may be encouraged to grow up a barrier to make use of every available piece of ground. Among the hill tribes of northern Thailand such barriers are known as 'edible' fences.

Fences

Fences give a garden a boundary and provide shelter. In Japanese gardens many kinds of fences are used traditionally, the aim being to convey a rustic ambience. In more recent years numerous English gardens have seen the return of the agricultural hurdle with the same intention.

ABOVE: *Willow 'wigwam' used to support climbing plants such as runner beans or sweet peas.*

ABOVE, LEFT: *A modern willow gardener's basket with pockets for trowels, forks and other horticultural equipment.*

BELOW, LEFT: *An open-ended basket made from buff and white willow; ideal for carrying long-stemmed flowers or loaves of bread.*

BELOW: *'The Garden of England'; a gardener in Kent, during Edwardian times (1901–1910), carrying a trug full of cut flowers.*

150

Hanging baskets

Baskets full of geraniums and petunias are hung around many British buildings in the summer, especially when garden space is restricted. The hemispherical containers are now most likely to be made of interlaced wire as metal can survive the load and the damp for a long time. Fashion has, however, brought about the return of the willow basket, although it is now quite likely to be woven over a wire skeleton.

Above, left: Hanging baskets outside a public house in the Cambridgeshire village of Histon.
Above, right: Japanese spring tine rake made from bamboo held in place with twined wires.
Left: A long, shallow English flower basket constructed from buff and brown willow.

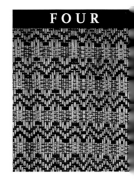

FOUR

Tools

Garden implements such as brooms and rakes are still made in many places using basketry techniques. Tools once made of bamboo may now be made of metal or plastic, but the techniques used to make them often remain the same.

Left: Fences and gates in a number of styles are considered an essential part of a Japanese garden.
Right: A makeshift wheelbarrow employed in tidying up a garden in southern Thailand.

PLANTS AND FLOWERS

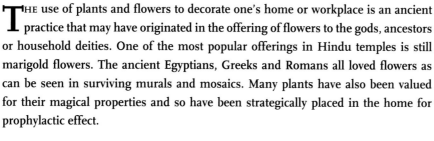

THE use of plants and flowers to decorate one's home or workplace is an ancient practice that may have originated in the offering of flowers to the gods, ancestors or household deities. One of the most popular offerings in Hindu temples is still marigold flowers. The ancient Egyptians, Greeks and Romans all loved flowers as can be seen in surviving murals and mosaics. Many plants have also been valued for their magical properties and so have been strategically placed in the home for prophylactic effect.

LEFT: *Novelty flower baskets shaped like ducks, owls, squirrels and many other whimsical shapes are made in China.*

RIGHT: *A Chinese flower vase made in Shanghai. The highly varnished casing of split bamboo hides a narrow glass cylinder which can hold water.*

BELOW: *Two stake and strand cache pots made in China from split bamboo. Baskets like these, intended for export, are frequently made in stacking sets.*

OPPOSITE, BELOW, LEFT: *A Japanese* ikebana *vase made from split bamboo. The flowers and water are placed in a large tube of bamboo culm concealed inside.*

OPPOSITE, BELOW, CENTRE: *A Japanese bamboo* ikebana *vase with a textured surface. The flowers are contained in a porcelain cylinder.*

OPPOSITE, BELOW, RIGHT: *British florists use a ring of twisted willow, into which flower stems can be inserted, as the foundation for garlands and wreaths.*

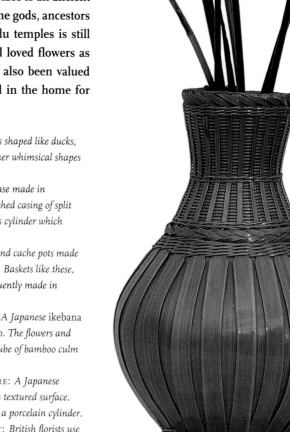

Cache pot

THE ideal receptacle for a plant is a ceramic pot which will retain soil and water. A cheap, ugly pot may be hidden inside a 'cache pot'. They are baskets made slightly bigger than standard-sized pots in a number of styles. Large numbers of trac-weave cocorib cache pots are now made in the Philippines for export.

Rush cache pots have often been constructed using a flower pot as the mould over which the rushes are plaited.

Flower arranging

AFTER centuries of civil strife, the seventeenth century heralded a period of peace and prosperity for the Japanese and, under the influence of Zen philosophy, a sophisticated simplicity was applied to arts and crafts. Flower arranging, or *ikebana*, became an artform in the hands of both women and men. Beautifully made baskets, which contain either a section of bamboo or a porcelain cylinder, are used to hold water for the flowers. These baskets often feature extraordinary textures and can be very valuable.

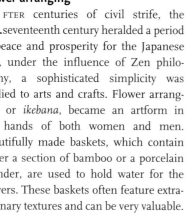

To suggest rustic charm, European florists favour small crudely made baskets, often with bark intact, for many of their arrangements. The baskets are filled with a block of water-retentive material into which flower stems can be pushed.

Wreaths

Wreaths for Christmas, funerals or other occasions may be created using a ring of twisted willow as a foundation into which the flower stems may be thrust. As the cut stems are deprived of water, longer-lasting arrangements depend on the use of evergreens or dried flowers.

ABOVE: *A Venetian flower seller with a long-handled flower basket.*
RIGHT: *Cache pot made by Ilocano basketmakers in the Philippines.*

IN THE HOME

BASKETRY has touched many aspects of domestic life, including storage, furniture, cleaning, the preparation of food, the covering of floors and even the construction of the house itself.

Housework

THE waste-paper basket is still a common feature of homes, classrooms and offices as an aid to tidiness. Formerly made of willow in a variety of openwork styles, waste-paper baskets constructed

RIGHT: *Two tightly woven willow laundry baskets made in Germany.*

LEFT: *Two Zulu grass floor brushes called* umshamelo. *The strands of grass are attached to a cord and then rolled up and bound with string, horsehair or plastic twine.*

BELOW, LEFT: *Chinese pillow of twill-plaited split bamboo.*

BELOW, CENTRE: *A twill-plaited grass holder for fire sticks; made by the Tutsi of Rwanda or Uganda.*

BOTTOM: *Balinese stake and strand baskets sold in England as wastepaper baskets.*

BELOW, RIGHT: *Sturdy log basket made from brown willow in French randing with buff willow waling.*

OPPOSITE, LEFT: *Rattan carpet beater. Many variations were available before the vacuum cleaner was in widespread use.*

OPPOSITE, TOP RIGHT: *Japanese stationery box made from split bamboo in plain-weave plaiting.*

from bamboo or rattan are now imported from Asia in large quantities.

For many, a vacuum cleaner is not an option, so the floor is swept with a brush or broom made from a bundle of twigs or grass stems which may be bound together in a complex or decorative manner.

Carpet beaters were widely used before the invention of the vacuum cleaner. In England, in Victorian and Edwardian times, rattan – since it was long and even – was bent and interlaced into many different designs.

Laundry

HUNDREDS of years ago good-quality clothes in Europe were made from linen and the term 'linen basket' is still used to describe a receptacle for soiled clothing. Once washed, the clean items are carried to and from the washing line in a 'laundry basket' traditionally made from willow, but more recently imitated in moulded plastic.

Storage

Anything from eggs to earrings can be stored in a basket. One of the toughest is the log basket for firewood which is most often made from willow, frequently with the bark intact.

Pets

Pampered pets are no longer the prerogative of the rich. Dogs and cats are treated as a member of the family in many homes in the West and provided with their own beds which are constructed to a standard design. Many pets have portable cages for taking them to the vet or on a journey, but these are now likely to be made of plastic or metal which are cheap and easy to clean.

Below: *Dog basket constructed from rattan rather than the traditional willow.*
Bottom: *Willow cat's travelling basket made in China.*

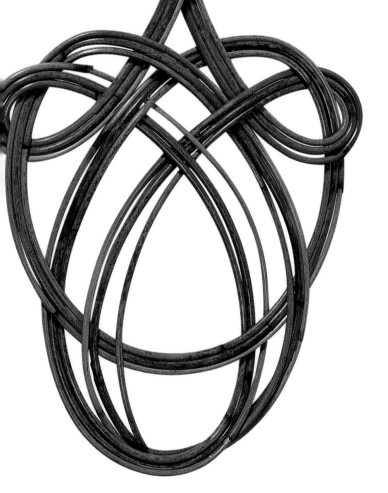

STORAGE

I<small>N</small> any society, items that are not in constant use must be stored, out of the way in a place from which they can be easily retrieved when needed. This keeps floor space as clear as possible and prevents the items getting damaged or spoilt. Anything from buttons to beans can be stored in basketry containers, some small enough to be carried in a sash around the body, others large enough for a person to stand up in.

Clothes

K<small>EEPING</small> clothing in a basket not only keeps it out of the way, but also protects it from dirt, smoke and pests. Many are constructed in a rectangular, hamper shape with a hinged lid, while others are cylindrical or urn shaped. Most baskets of this type have a lid, a wide neck and a foot to keep their contents out of the damp.

The vanity of the owner is often reflected in the decoration of the container as well as its contents. One particularly fine example is the *keben*, a square Balinese basket of plaited bamboo, which is sometimes painted. Another beautiful version made from split bamboo can be found in the city of Chiang Mai in northern Thailand.

Foodstuffs

T<small>HE</small> largest storage containers of all are those used to store grain, beans and other dry foodstuffs for communal use. A tribal community in India or Africa may have several of these, each for a different food – rice, millet, beans, lentils and so on.

FOUR

A strong framework of interwoven rods is built on a platform close to the villagers' houses and, for added protection from rain, rats and insects, is often coated in mud or dung. The Native Americans of California and the Southwest made large storage baskets with the coiling technique. Sometimes it was necessary for the weaver to sit inside the basket to accomplish this task.

Smaller quantities of foodstuffs may be stored in the home. In the southwestern region of North America many tribes made beautifully decorated, closely worked baskets for this purpose. The grain baskets or *ollas* made by the White Mountain Apache were of such fine workmanship that they became a trade item and now sell to collectors for huge prices.

OPPOSITE, TOP LEFT: *Turkish white willow basket used to store clothes.*
OPPOSITE, CENTRE LEFT: *Yucca-sewn olla made by the Pima of southern Arizona.*
OPPOSITE, BOTTOM LEFT: *Coiled basket acquired as Barotse from Zambia.*
OPPOSITE, ABOVE, RIGHT: *Double-walled split bamboo basket made in Chiang Mai, northern Thailand.*
OPPOSITE, BOTTOM RIGHT: *Rattan stake and strand storage basket from Lombok.*

ABOVE: *Large Tutsi storage basket, from Burundi, stitched with raffia bamboo (1 metre, 3 ft high).*
ABOVE, RIGHT: *Western Apache olla for storing grain; it has a three-rod bunched foundation sewn with willow and devil's claw.*
RIGHT: *Enormous grain storage baskets at a village in Lesotho.*

PERSONAL STORAGE

Iᴛᴇᴍs for personal use, whether cosmetic, spiritual or work related, are frequently stored in containers upon which special attention has been lavished.

Work baskets

Tᴀsᴋs that traditionally demanded a great deal of a woman's time such as sewing, knitting and mending require specialist equipment and materials that must be easily accessible. Sewing baskets come in various sizes, sometimes divided into sections to keep threads and tools separate and usually with padding under the lid for needles. Wool baskets, on the other hand, are larger and may have a comparatively narrow opening.

Women's trinket baskets

Sᴍᴀʟʟ baskets are frequently used as receptacles for objects for personal use such as cosmetics, jewelry and other valuables, and are often elaborately decorated. In Indochina this may take the form of cylindrical basketry pots with lacquered decoration, but in most places the usual form is potbellied with a fitted lid.

Aʙᴏᴠᴇ ᴀɴᴅ ᴄᴇɴᴛʀᴇ: Sᴇᴡɪɴɢ ʙᴀsᴋᴇᴛs ꜰʀᴏᴍ ᴛʜᴇ 1927/28 ᴄᴀᴛᴀʟᴏɢᴜᴇ ᴏꜰ Hᴀʟʟ & Aɴᴅᴇʀsᴏɴ Lᴛᴅ, Cᴀʟᴄᴜᴛᴛᴀ, Iɴᴅɪᴀ

Aʙᴏᴠᴇ: *'Telescoping' bag made in Luzon, the Philippines.*
Tᴏᴘ, ʀɪɢʜᴛ: *Nineteenth-century willow sewing basket; probably French.*

Aʙᴏᴠᴇ, ᴍɪᴅᴅʟᴇ: *Navajo wool-stitched trinket basket made by Delphina Gray.*
Rɪɢʜᴛ: *Basket for wool; made from bamboo and plaited rice straw.*

Men's paraphernalia containers

Iɴ places as far apart as Myanmar (Burma), the Philippines, the Amazon jungle and the Papago reservations of southern Arizona men carry 'telescoping' pouches of plaited cane. They are long and narrow with a lid that overlaps the bottom sufficiently to allow for considerable variation in the quantity of their contents. They are used to carry tobacco, betel nut for chewing, medicine or items, such as paint and feathers, intended for self adornment or ceremonial use. This form of basket is also widely favoured by shamen for carrying the specialist tools of their trade.

Among the Arhuaca and Kogi Indians of the Sierra Nevada de Santa Marta region of Colombia, a man's costume includes a pair of *mochilas*, bags of interlooped agave fibre, worn one over each shoulder across the body. One is for everyday essentials, while the other contains the omnipresent coca leaves.

Top ʟᴇꜰᴛ: *Hmong girl, in the hills of northern Thailand, using a sewing basket of woven plastic.*
Aʙᴏᴠᴇ: *Nineteenth-century Japanese plaited box in the* mingei *(folk art) style.*
Top ʀɪɢʜᴛ: *Twill-plaited, skeined willow shoulder bag made by German basketmaker Michael Thierschmann.*
Rɪɢʜᴛ: *Twined raffia pouches from Abomey, the capital of Dahomey, now Benin.*

FOUR

FURNITURE

Chairs and other items of furniture have been constructed using basketmaking techniques for thousands of years. Beds and chairs upholstered with matting or leather thonging were found in tombs of the Egyptian Eighteenth Dynasty (1550–1069 BC), while the Etruscans (pre 400 BC) strung their beds with interlaced metal strips. The sarcophagi of Roman matrons were often carved with scenes of daily life and one recurring motif is a woman seated in a wicker chair while a servant dresses her hair. Today, some furniture is made entirely of basketwork, but many chairs have a solid frame and only the seat is interlaced.

FOUR

Wicker furniture

Wicker furniture was once made in many parts of Europe, but rattan centre cane has now become much more common. A huge number of rattan chairs and sofas are now constructed in Southeast Asia for export to the West where they have become fashionable as conservatory furniture.

One unique English item is the Somerset chair which has a frame of hazel or willow and a back and seat of willow basketry.

ABOVE: *Imported cane furniture destined for use in an English conservatory.*
TOP RIGHT: *Wicker chair made in Eastern Europe.*
RIGHT: *Grass and twine chair made in northeast India.*

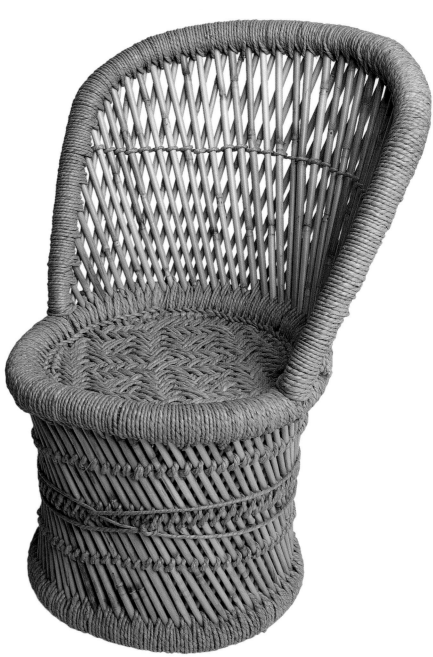

twilled patterns to make the bottoms of chairs and charpoys in northwest India, Pakistan and Afghanistan.

Split-cane seating, now universally popular, was introduced to Europe from India during the reign of Charles II in the seventeenth century. The rattan cane is generally threaded through holes in the frame and then interlaced in three or four directions.

Assembly

THE British raj led to the creation of a furniture industry in the Indian subcontinent with the making of rattan chairs, stools, tables, screens and beds. Frames are made from whole cane which is bent into the right shape after it has been heated with a blow torch to soften it. Separate sections are fixed together with nails, joinery or split-cane lashings.

In northeastern India tubular stools called *mudah* or *mura* are constructed from split bamboo or tough grasses. Rigidity is provided by two sets of splints that cross on opposite diagonals to brace each other.

Seating

RUSH has been used in England since the Middle Ages, if not earlier, to provide a more comfortable seat than solid wood. In other parts of Europe straw, sedge or marram grass have also been used.

Rawhide or twine made from jute, hemp or sisal is interlaced in checks or

ABOVE, LEFT: *Moroccan cane table.*
LEFT: *Making willow chairs at a workshop in Bavaria, southern Germany.*
ABOVE, CENTRE: *Carved chair from Shekavati in the Indian state of Rajasthan. The seat is woven from jute twine.*
TOP RIGHT: *Carved chair, from the Swat Valley in Pakistan, with a seat of interlaced rawhide.*
CENTRE RIGHT: *Traditional English country chair made from green ash with a rush seat.*
BOTTOM RIGHT: *The early stages of weaving seating from rushes.*

MATTING

WHEN Russian seafarers visited Tahiti in the early 1800s they were offered a large pandanus mat for trade. The chief told them that this was the finest object their craftsmen could produce.

Mats are an indispensable item in the lives of many in undeveloped regions where they often serve several of the same functions as textiles. Matting may be used as a floor covering, as walls or room dividers, as a roof for a house, as a boat or cart and even as clothing. Mats are also used as a surface on which agricultural produce can be spread out to dry or, in Turkey and Central Asia, on which damp wool can be arranged and rolled up during the manufacture of felt.

In the communal longhouses of the Amazon Basin or Borneo a mat placed on the floor is one of the few ways in which an individual can define personal space.

Matting may be coarse and tough for everyday wear and tear or fine and decorative for sleeping on or for ceremonial use.

Coiled mats

LARGE mats are often made by coiling plaited grass or straw into circles or ellipses with concentric patterns. They may be colourful, like those created in Zanzibar, or in subdued natural tones like those from South Africa. In West Bengal durable mats are made from coarse jute fibres which became popular in the West during the 1960s as doormats.

Plaited mats

SOME of the finest mats of all are those woven from palm, pandanus or split rattan in the Malay Archipelago, the Philippines and Borneo. These are twill plaited on the diagonal in two or more colours. Some mats from eastern Malaya are woven in complex patterns from thin strips of dyed pandanus; they are so fine they resemble textiles.

Twined mats

TWINED mats are popular in parts of Africa where the twining runs the length of the mat. The passive elements may be of grass or reed. The nomadic Tuareg use leather strips twined decoratively round reeds.

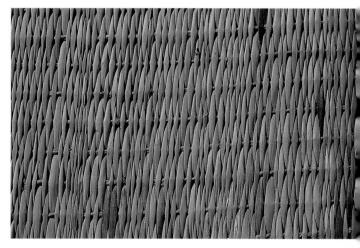

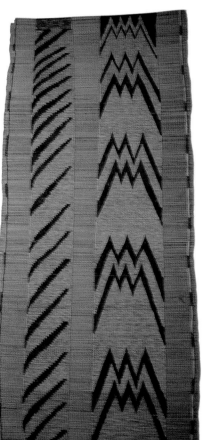

OPPOSITE, RIGHT, CENTRE: *Weaving a Turkish rush mat.*

OPPOSITE, BOTTOM RIGHT: *Ojibway girl, from the American Great Lakes, sitting on a cattail mat.*

ABOVE, LEFT: *Large Penan sitting mat, from Sarawak, plaited from split rattan in the 'curved snake' pattern. They are sometimes woven tightly enough to be watertight.*

ABOVE, RIGHT: *Colourful mat constructed in Zanzibar from coiled plaits with an anchoring cord.*

LEFT: *Fine reed mat or screen made by the Tutsi of Rwanda in around 1900.*

RIGHT: *Rush matting employed in Turkey as an underlay for kilim rugs.*

BELOW: *A reed and leather mat from Mauritania used by the nomadic Tuareg of the Sahara desert.*

Woven mats

MANY mats are woven in a plain weave using a fibre warp to bind stiff wefts. This is the method used in Turkey and Central Asia where a simple loom is often employed to facilitate the process.

OPPOSITE TOP: *Nineteenth-century Kurdish reed screen from Turkey.*

OPPOSITE, FAR LEFT: *Zulu coiled plait grass mat.*

SMALL MATS

Small mats are made utilizing construction methods similar to those used to make large ones, and often for similar purposes. In Sarawak, for example, a miniature mat was hung from the back of a man's belt to provide a clean, dry place for him to sit when working in the jungle. Small mats one metre square, or smaller, may provide not only a place to sit, but a portable work surface. In Japan artists carried their brushes rolled up in a mat of bamboo splints.

By far the most common use of small mats is in association with food.

Preparing food

Mats may be used when gathering and drying foodstuffs, and then, in the case of the twined Zulu *isithebe*, they may be placed under a quern to catch ground meal.

In eastern Turkey flat loaves are still baked weekly and stacked on a large coiled mat made from reeds. They are covered with a cloth and periodically sprinkled with water to keep them fresh.

In Japan, where the presentation of food is highly important, rice or sushi is sometimes made into neat cylinders by rolling it up in a mat.

The Spanish use a mat of coiled esparto grass to strain the oil pressed from olives.

LEFT: *Zulu* isithebe *used when collecting and processing food, Hlubi sub-tribe.*
TOP RIGHT: *Coiled reed bread mat from Gaziantep, eastern Turkey (70 cm, 27½ in., across).*
UPPER RIGHT: *Willow stake and strand platter made in France (30 cm, 12 in.).*
LOWER RIGHT: *Coiled mat from the Horn of Africa (48 cm, 19 in.).*
BOTTOM RIGHT: *Large coiled eating mat from the Sudan (77 cm, 30 in., across).*

In many countries a mat may be employed instead of a table, with a family and their guests seated around it on the floor.

FOUR

On the table

Mats are used all around the world to define an individual place setting and provide a clean surface on which to eat. They also protect the surface of a table from damage caused by hot kettles and cooking pans.

Cleanliness is next to godliness

For those who are on the move or cannot afford a rug, a mat often serves as a convenient substitute when a clean place is required for prayer. Devout Muslims must pray in a clean place five times a day.

ABOVE: *Three coiled mats for covering water pots; made in Mali or Niger (28 cm, 11 in., across).*

RIGHT: *Plaited pandanus mats from Aceh in Sumatra (45 x 45 cm, 18 in. x 18 in.).*

BELOW: *Coiled esparto grass mat, from Spain, used to press olive oil (30 cm, 12 in., across). As coiling has progressed, each new turn has been ingeniously attached by incorporating fibres protruding from the previous one.*

OPPOSITE, BOTTOM LEFT: *Plaited birch bark mat from Archangel, Russia (28 cm, 11 in., long).*

B ASKETRY is used in many aspects of the preparation and serving of meals. The gift of a basket of fruit to a sick friend or relative is a European tradition that can be traced back to Roman times.

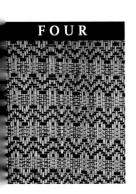

FOUR

TOP, LEFT: *Catalonian pair of baskets for peeling potatoes, made by Lluis Grau.*
TOP, RIGHT: *A bamboo rice steamer from Gunung Kidung village near Yogyakarta, Java.*
ABOVE: *Irish* sciathóg *for straining potatoes, made from willow by Alison Fitzgerald.*

Storage

T IGHTLY woven baskets are used all around the world to store dried foods. Perishable produce, on the other hand, is stored in loosely woven or openwork baskets that allow the circulation of air. In France, spherical wire baskets are made to hold eggs, while garlic bulbs may be kept in a basket made from garlic stems.

Liquids stored in clay or metal pots are often covered with round mats or small basketry bowls such as the Zulu *imbenge*.

Preparation

I N many villages around the world the day begins with women and girls pounding grain and then sieving or winnowing it to remove the husks. They then grind it into meal, sift it and start to cook.

Fruit and vegetables must be washed, peeled, rinsed and drained, all processes that require the use of baskets.

Cooking

A LTHOUGH vegetable-fibre baskets cannot be exposed to direct flames, they may be used to immerse food in boiling water or to hold it above steam. In Japan and China bamboo steaming baskets are stacked one above another, each containing a different item. Wire baskets, on the other hand, such as the English chip pan or the Chinese noodle dipper, are not damaged by flames or boiling oil.

Native American tribes actually cooked in baskets in two ways – parching trays were filled with seeds or acorns and roasted by adding hot sand or stones, and waterproof baskets were used as saucepans by filling them with water into which red hot stones were dropped to bring the water to the boil. In Southeast Asia rice is often wrapped in interlaced leaves and immersed in boiling water.

ABOVE, LEFT: *Tutsi reed screen from Rwanda. Screens like this are set up around a platform to provide shade for sacred milk pots.*
ABOVE, RIGHT: *Split bamboo winnowing trays from Thailand (left) and Nepal (right).*
RIGHT: *Ladles and strainers from India, Japan and China.*

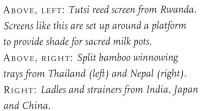

Once cooked, food may be strained in an open mesh basket or placed on a loosely woven tray to drain.

Serving

In most cultures mats may be used to keep food clean or to protect the table. Bread is often placed on the table in baskets and other foodstuffs can be protected from flies by a basketwork dome.

INSET, ABOVE, RIGHT: *Atayal women from Taiwan pounding meal. Several baskets involved in the preparation of foodstuffs can be seen in the photograph, notably a large twill-plaited winnowing tray in the foreground.*
RIGHT: *A conical food cover from Ethiopia or the Sudan, where it is essential to protect food from flies. The decoration is created through the dense stitching of coiled grass bundles.*

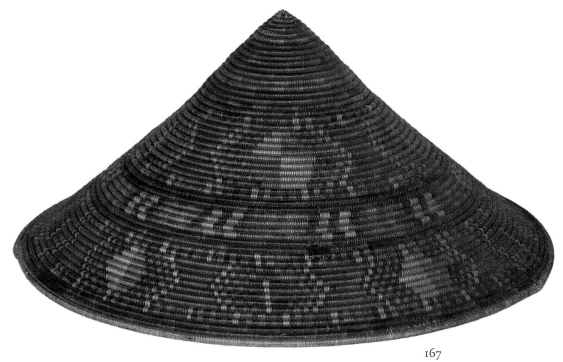

CARRYING WATER

Fetching and carrying water has always been an important task and in parts of Africa may still demand several hours walking a day. Storing the precious water and other liquids, such as milk or beer, is also a crucial problem. Societies that lack the technology to make metal or ceramic jugs and pots have solved the problem in a number of ways using basketry.

Bark

In the forests of Northern Europe, Siberia and North America, and in the wilderness of Australia instant cups have long been made from folded bark. Sometimes more permanent vessels are plaited from strips or sewn together from sheets. Koumiss (mare's milk) buckets are carefully made with elaborate stitching and decoration.

Resin

In Southeast Asia baskets are coated in lacquer, while in the Southwest of the USA Native Americans traditionally coat their baskets with pitch from the piñon pine. The pitch is smeared inside and out – on the inside it is kept soft and spreads more easily by rolling a hot stone around.

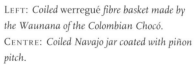

Left: *Coiled werregué fibre basket made by the Waunana of the Colombian Chocó.*
Centre: *Coiled Navajo jar coated with piñon pitch.*
Top right: *Apache girl with water jar; photographed by Frank Randall in 1885.*
Right, centre: *Western Apache twined jar awaiting a coating of pitch; made by Charlene Lupe.*
Right: *Watertight basket of coiled ilala palm from KwaZulu, South Africa.*

Gourds

Gourds make ideal containers for water, milk or beer, but are prone to cracking when dropped. To protect them from damage they may be wrapped in a skin of interwoven grass, cane or leather. In the Horn of Africa milk bottles are so well covered that it is difficult to see the gourd.

Swollen fibres

The most impressive waterproof baskets are without a doubt those that are woven so tightly, using absorbent fibres that swell up when wet, that they do not leak. The Zulus weave a coiled waterpot called an *isichumo* from ilala palm folioles or dwarf strelitzia fibre. The *shigras* of Ecuador, made from inter-looped agave fibre, were originally used for carrying water, but are now made mainly for tourists and may well leak.

BELOW: Shigra *made in Ecuador from looped agave fibre.*
RIGHT: *Ethiopian waterpot made from a gourd protected with a layer of coiled grasses and decorated with cowrie shells.*

FOUR

169

LUNCH BOXES AND PICNIC BASKETS

In the middle of the day many workers around the world take a short break and have a bite to eat, however humble. Often it is packed in a special basket. Lunch boxes are sometimes referred to as tiffin baskets after the Anglo-Indian word for a light meal. Food carried to a picnic or a party also needs a suitable container to keep it safe and is usually carried in a lidded basket with a handle.

Rice baskets

RICE is the staple food in Southeast Asia and the whole day's quota is often cooked first thing in the morning. Portions are laddled out into baskets that hang from the shoulder by a cord and are carried off to work. The same basic design exists from Assam to the Philippines. In Thailand this rice basket or *kong khao* is fitted with a wooden foot to keep its contents clean and dry.

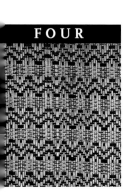

LEFT: *Plaited container for cooked rice; made in Abra in the northern Philippines.*
ABOVE: Kong khao, *a Thai container for cooked rice.*

A distinctive rice basket found in Bhutan and neighbouring Arunachal Pradesh is made of two semi-spherical sections about 20 cm (8 in.) across that fit very tightly together. In Arunachal Pradesh they are called *bunchungs* and are made of plaited bamboo splints, but in Bhutan brightly dyed reeds are used.

Chinese baskets

THE Chinese transport meals of several courses or gifts of food in a set of stacking baskets held together by a handle. These baskets are often beautifully lacquered or painted and come in a range of styles. In Fukien, for instance, they are round, while others from Ningbo may be square.

Picnic baskets

IN Europe and the USA most picnic baskets belong to one of two types. The first is a wicker (or in the USA probably a splint) basket carried by a handle on the arm or in the hand and fitted with a pair of lids hinged in the middle. The other is the more capacious hamper shaped like a suitcase and fitted on the inside with receptacles for crockery and cutlery as well as for food and drink.

OPPOSITE, TOP: *Bhutanese portable container for cooked rice; made of plaited bamboo strips.*
ABOVE, LEFT: *Willow drop-lid hamper made by G. W. Scott and Sons of London in the 1930s.*
TOP RIGHT: *Modern picnic hamper made for export in the Philippines.*
CENTRE, RIGHT: *Oak splint lunch basket in a style developed by colonists in Pennsylvania, USA.*
NEAR RIGHT: *Chinese stacking food basket from Fukien, China, made from lacquered basketry.*
FAR RIGHT: *Plaited and painted food baskets from Ningbo, Zhejiang, China.*

SPIRITUAL AND CEREMONIAL BASKETS

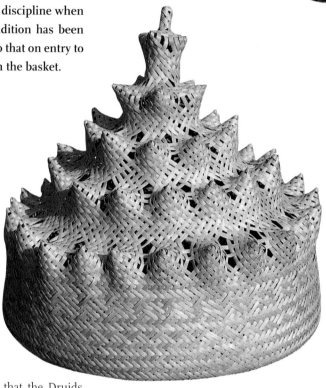

BASKETS play an active role – as container, teacher or even therapist – in both the mundane and the spiritual life of people from many cultures. For Native Americans, the Navajo wedding basket and the Pima and Papago 'man in the maze' baskets remind the beholder of the need for determination and self discipline when treading life's turbulent road, while the Apache burden basket tradition has been adopted by many non-Native Americans. It is hung at the doorway so that on entry to the house a visitor may unburden himself and leave his negativity in the basket.

Offerings

FROM time immemorial divine offerings have been made in baskets, as recorded in Deuteronomy 26; 2, 4. Ancient stone carvings from Sumeria depict the priest-kings carrying baskets of building materials on their heads to sanctify the laying of the foundations of new temples.

To this day, a coiled shallow basket with a pronounced foot is used to present offerings at shrines in Thailand. On it are placed fruit, flowers and incense. On Bali, in the early morning, young women prepare similar offerings on trays of interlaced leaves and place them at strategic positions on the pavement outside houses and shops, at crossroads and so on to placate the spirits. On more formal occasions, trays of offerings may be piled high on mats inside an enclosure made of freshly plaited palm leaves.

Julius Caesar claimed that the Druids in Britain made human sacrifices, burning their victims in giant wickerwork statues. In Western Europe the burning of wicker figures, sometimes as large as

TOP: *A Kuba shaman's rattle from the Democratic Republic of Congo.*

ABOVE, LEFT: *In animist societies all around the world magical paraphernalia is kept in containers similar to this koppit from the Philippines.*

ABOVE, RIGHT: *A ceremonial Iban hat from Sarawak. The protrusions represent abundance and fertility.*

LEFT: *David Goff Eveleigh setting fire to a wicker giant at a modern 'Fire Festival'.*

OPPOSITE, TOP LEFT: *A modern twined Apache burden basket for sale on the Fort Apache Indian Reservation.*

OPPOSITE, TOP CENTRE: *A Papago (Tohono O'odham) 'man in the maze' basket. The ancestor hero Elder Brother is at the entrance.*

OPPOSITE, TOP RIGHT: *Coiled sikki grass statue of the Hindu god Ganesh; made in Bihar, India.*

15 metres (49 ft) high, was indeed a part of festivities at Midsummer until the eighteenth century.

Corn dollies

IN Greece, Mexico, Russia, Scandinavia, Germany and Ireland animals, favours and figures are made from straw at harvest time and Christmas. In England these small sculptures are known as corn dollies. It has been suggested that this is a corruption of 'idol' as the figures may represent the deity of the corn. Traditionally, a field was harvested in ever-decreasing circles so that all the magic power would be trapped in the final sheaf. This was cut with much ceremony and a cage was woven from the straw in which the corn god was imprisoned until the next crop was sewn. The shapes, bells, horseshoes, crossed keys, etc., varied from county to county.

ABOVE: *The Crossed Keys of St Peter, one of the many English variations of the corn dolly.*

FAR LEFT: *The Bridget Cross, an Irish version of the corn dolly.*
NEAR LEFT: *Here, in Belgium, a man is re-enacting Joseph's journey to present Christ at the Temple, carrying an offering of doves in a cage.*
ABOVE: *Two Balinese palm figures representing the rice goddess, Dewi Sri.*

Growing up

IN the Native American Hopi society from the day children are born until puberty they are presented with small plaques made by their paternal aunt or grandmother as gifts from the Katchinas, the spirits. Playing with these helps establish the child's identification with the spirit world and the society into which he or she has been born.

The umbilical cord is an object of reverence in some parts of the Pacific and may be kept, carefully stored in a specially made plaited tube.

Puberty

A GIRL'S first menstrual flow, her entry into womanhood, is widely celebrated in Native American cultures. An Apache girl's 'Sunrise', for instance, involves her running around a course marked out with baskets and finally being showered with gifts from a burden basket.

The basket has, in fact, been adopted worldwide as a symbol of womanhood and nourishment. Basket dances continue to be a regular part of the spiritual life of Hopi women's societies. Much of the significance is kept secret, but at the climax baskets are thrown to the watching men who fight fiercely to win one.

FOUR

Making a first basket

IN some Native American communities children are taught the skills of basket-making from a very early age, often imitating their mothers at work, but other societies ban children from the craft until after puberty. In tribes such as the Barasana of the Northwest Amazon elders teach the making of baskets as part of the male initiation rites.

OPPOSITE, ABOVE: *Hopi coiled plaque from Second Mesa, Arizona. Baskets remain a significant part of the Hopi people's religion and plaques are presented to individuals at many important times in their life relating to spiritual development.*
OPPOSITE, BELOW, LEFT: *An old twined Apache burden basket of the type used at 'Sunrise' ceremonies.*
OPPOSITE, BELOW, RIGHT: *Maori kete made from New Zealand flax, known to the Maori as harakeke.*

In New Zealand the *kete*, a soft plaited basket made from New Zealand flax (*Phormium tenax*) has become a symbol of cultural identity to such an extent that all Maori children are now taught how to weave one as part of the curriculum. The *kete whakairo* may be woven in a range of colours and patterns that require skill and patience and are subsequently treated with pride and respect.

Initiation

THE ceremonies accompanying initiation into religious societies often involve baskets. The Mysteries at Eleusis, which probably date back to 1356 BC, were attended by large numbers of Athenians. The rituals included transferring secret articles between boxes and baskets. On the fourteenth day a great procession took place in which the kalaqos, the sacred basket of Demeter, was paraded before the initiates in a consecrated cart.

ABOVE, LEFT, INSET: *An Apache girl being showered with gifts at her 'Sunrise'.*
ABOVE: *Elaborate kete whakairos such as this one have become a symbol of Maori identity.*
ABOVE, RIGHT, INSET: *A workshop teaching Maori basketmaking skills.*
BELOW: *These newly initiated boys from Yamai village, Papua New Guinea, have returned from a month in the bush bearing baskets they have made.*

ROMAN COIN SHOWING DEMETER'S BASKET BEING PARADED DURING THE FESTIVAL AT ELEUSIS, NEAR ATHENS, GREECE

WEDDINGS

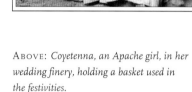

S INCE ancient times basketry has been associated with many stages of a couple's courtship, from the early stages of wooing to the celebration of marriage.

Courtship

I N Khonoma village in Nagaland, India, the *kophi*, a beautiful flaring burden basket of the Angami Nagas, is given to a woman by a man as a sign of his commitment to marry her.

In Germany the phrase 'to give a basket', '*einen Korb geben*', once meant to spurn a suitor. Until the end of the eighteenth century women would lower a basket from their windows to receive gifts from their sweethearts. If the suitor was unwelcome the girl would lower a basket with a loose bottom so that the present would fall out.

The wedding

T HE wedding basket is the most distinctive of the Navajo baskets. The patterns woven into it are intended to represent the stormy nature of life through which there is a path leading out. At the wedding holy corn pollen is piled high on the basket by a shaman and eaten by the happy couple and guests. The

ABOVE: *Coyetenna, an Apache girl, in her wedding finery, holding a basket used in the festivities.*
LEFT: *The patterns on this Zulu basket record information about the bride's dowry and good wishes for her future.*
BELOW, LEFT: *Wheatstraw mats used to place food on and as gifts at Syrian weddings.*
BELOW: *Teo Chow wedding basket from Guangdong province, China.*
OPPOSITE, LEFT AND CENTRE: *Messob, or marriage table, commissioned by a bride's family in Shoa district, Ethiopia (85 cm, 33½ in., high).*

RIGHT: *Bobo wedding baskets from Mali.*
BOTTOM: *Hopi wedding baskets displayed as they might be when given by the bride's family to the groom's family.*

In Mali a Bobo bride is presented with a set of stacking baskets. Each contains a different grain or seed and represents everything she could possibly need in her new life.

In Germany, in living memory, a bride was given a special basket, often brightly painted and full of useful gifts, by her godmother. Family rivalry frequently meant that a cart was delivered on a bride's wedding day loaded with baskets vying with each other in the extravagance of their contents and decoration.

FOUR

person who eats the last mouthful is allowed to keep the basket.

Beautiful trays of coiled dyed wheat-straw, 20 cm (8 in.) or more across, are made in Syria for the serving of food at the wedding breakfast.

Wedding gifts

A GROOM'S family give supplies and clothes for a Hopi wedding and in return the bride's family make a quantity of baskets and plaques of a reciprocal value, a task that often takes years. Many of these may be given away later or sold, but the groom will take his with him to the grave. Without it he would not gain admittance to the spirit world.

... TO THE GRAVE

THE association of baskets with death and the afterlife goes back to prehistory. The very word 'coffin' is derived from the Greek kofinos which means 'a basket'.

Execution and sacrifice

FROM the thirteenth to the early nineteenth centuries the English ritual execution of hanging, drawing and quartering included dragging heretics and traitors to their place of execution on a wicker hurdle. During the French Revolution in the eighteenth century the decapitated bodies of royalists, including the king himself, were rolled into a long, lidded basket beside the guillotine.

A receptacle for the body

IN many parts of Mexico babies are born on plaited palm or rush mats called *petates*. These same mats will one day form the shrouds in which they will be buried, a custom dating back centuries to their ancestors the Mixtec. The inhabitants of the Aleutian Islands off Alaska also once wrapped their dead in matting made from grasses and left them to be mummified in dry caves on the slopes of volcanoes. Ancient Egyptian coffins made of coiled basketry and dating back to before the pyramids were built (10,000–8,000 BC) were discovered by William Flinders Petrie

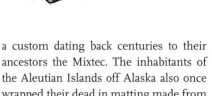

ABOVE: *Korean mourners once shaded their heads with enormous straw hats, sometimes for several years.*
LEFT: *Painted basket, from Hedesunda in the Swedish province of Gästrikland, used to carry food to both weddings and funerals.*
FAR LEFT: *Painted basket from Hälsingland, Sweden.*
OPPOSITE, TOP LEFT: *The plaque presented to a Hopi bridegroom is his passport to the spirit world.*
OPPOSITE, TOP RIGHT: *'Gift' or 'jewel' baskets, covered with feathers, are a speciality of the Californian Pomo. The baskets' most important function was their destruction in honour of the dead.*
OPPOSITE, CENTRE: *Offerings of food have been made on baskets since before the time of the Pharaohs in Egypt and in some parts of the world the custom continues.*
OPPOSITE, BOTTOM: *Willow coffin made by Trevor Leat, a basketmaker working at Castle Douglas in Scotland. Wicker coffins were used in the nineteenth century for paupers' burials, but with the increase in woodland and environmentally friendly burials, the use of basketry coffins is seeing a revival.*

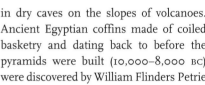

in the desert south of Cairo. The Incas, too, employed baskets in their funeral rights. Many mummies dating from before AD 200 have been discovered in the dry climate of the Paracas peninsular in Peru wrapped in layers of gorgeous textiles. The bodies were seated in shallow basketwork trays or bound with plaited ropes that, in effect, formed a coiled basket.

The burials of the Anasazi and Utes of Utah and the Four Corners Country of the USA were much humbler. The bodies of men, women and dogs have all been found, tenderly covered with baskets, in caves in canyon walls.

AN INCA MUMMY BUNDLE IN A COILED ROPE WRAPPING

Burial goods

IN Cave du Pont in Utah the bottoms of the burial baskets had been deliberately broken. They had been 'killed' so that their owners would be able to use them in the spirit world. An alternate way of sending the baskets ahead was practised by the Native Americans of southern California who danced around a fierce bonfire into which they finally threw the baskets. Even the feathered 'jewel' baskets of the Pomo were sacrificed in this way.

Virtually all ancient cultures buried their dead with useful equipment for their next life. The Egyptian king Tutankhamun himself had a plentiful supply of basketwork.

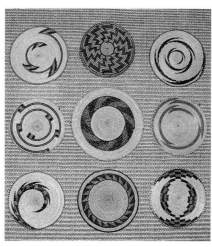

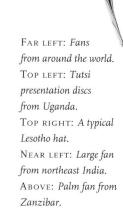

FAR LEFT: *Fans from around the world.*
TOP LEFT: *Tutsi presentation discs from Uganda.*
TOP RIGHT: *A typical Lesotho hat.*
NEAR LEFT: *Large fan from northeast India.*
ABOVE: *Palm fan from Zanzibar.*

FIVE

THE WORLD AT YOUR FINGERTIPS

WIDER APPLICATIONS OF BASKETRY

LEFT: *A house in Samoa built like an inverted basket.*
RIGHT: *A whimsical storage chest made in Turkey.*

THE idea that we must confine ourselves by labels is an academic and artificial luxury self imposed by modern societies. Questions like 'what is a basket?' have no relevance to people who are using the skills they have acquired to survive. So if a problem can be solved through the application of basketry methods, there is no longer a problem. The fact that an object needed – be it boat, bridge or building – is not technically a 'basket' does not prevent the use of basketmaking skills.

NECESSITY IS THE MOTHER OF INVENTION

EARLY hunter-gatherers made containers as needed from the materials to hand and so subsequent generations have applied their skills to many problems. As protection against the elements, palm leaf hats and birch bark shoes were made –

ENGLISH BASKET SELLER WITH HATS AND FANS, AFTER A WOODBLOCK PRINT OF 1640

FIVE

ABOVE: *A woman in a village in the Nepalese hills demonstrating a hex-weave rain shield worn while working in the fields.*
RIGHT: *Zandé spearmen who, armed with spears and basketry shields, conquered the Mangbettus of what is now the Democratic Republic of Congo during the late nineteenth century.*

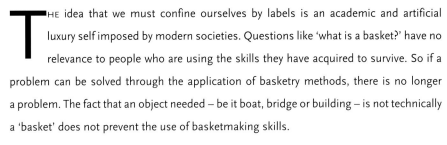

RIGHT: *Taman bamboo hat, Putussibau, Kalimantan.*
BELOW, LEFT: *Javanese* becak *driver in a rain hat, Yogyakarta.*

an imaginative manipulation of the materials to hand. More permanent protection was created in the form of simple buildings which were in essence large inverted baskets.

Different environments pose different problems and solutions. For example, reed boats made it possible to go fishing in an environment with few trees. Survival is a powerful muse.

RISING TO THE OCCASION

Basketmaking is often viewed by the uninitiated as a humble craft, but its techniques have been applied to many ambitious projects. Slung from a balloon in a basket, mankind has floated high above the earth and the stones used to build the great European cathedrals were hoisted aloft in baskets. In the eighteenth century when the spires of London churches toppled they were repaired with the aid of wickerwork scaffolding. It is not with stone that the deepest chasms of the Himalayas and the Andes are bridged, but with rope, bamboo and basketry.

FAR LEFT: *Picking spinach from bamboo boats in China.*
NEAR LEFT: *Korean shoe salesman.*
ABOVE: *Rajasthani wedding cart with interlaced metal roof.*

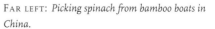

183

ARCHITECTURE

BASKETS have often been used in the building process, for fetching and carrying, and they have also frequently been used to form the structure of the building itself.

Living in a basket

MANY crude dwellings erected by nomadic or semi-nomadic people resemble upturned baskets. Poles are thrust into the ground and lashed together at the top to make a cone, like an Apache *wickiup*, or bent over to form a dome or tunnel, like an Australian aborigine *bender*. The framework formed is then covered with interlaced boughs, layers of bark, thatch or palm fronds. Some structures of this type built in Samoa or KwaZulu are large enough to accommodate hundreds of people. The traditional dwelling of the Marsh Arabs of southern Iraq, built out of huge bundles of *qasab* reed, could be 20 metres (66 ft) long and 6 metres (20 ft) high.

TOP, RIGHT: *Jat caste housing unit in Binasar in the Churu district of Rajasthan in India. The wattle walls are ready for covering with mud and dung.*
RIGHT: *Woven palm fronds used as fence and wall panels at a house compound in Zanzibar.*
BELOW, LEFT: *The walls of a house in Laos which were made by plaiting strips of flattened bamboo.*
BELOW, RIGHT: *A Polynesian home on the island of Ong Tong Java with wall panels plaited from pandanus strips.*

Roofs and walls

IN hotter climates matting or panels of interlaced bamboo or reed provide adequate, easily assembled walls and roofs. Reasonably rainproof roofs can be constructed from palm fronds. They can be folded along the rib and the two sides plaited together.

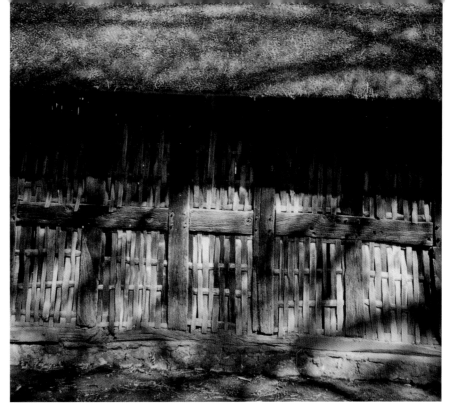

Before roofing felt became available, English thatchers lined their roofs with square mats called *fleekins* made from woven bundles of reed which prevented the thatch falling through the joists.

Solid walls may be built from wattle and daub. Although this is an English term describing panels of interlaced hazel rods plastered with clay, the same method is employed using mud or cow dung in many parts of Africa and India.

The yurt

T HE *yurt* is an easily transportable dwelling found in Central Asia and Mongolia (where it is called a *ger*). It can

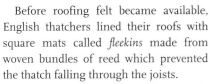

ABOVE, LEFT: *Reed roof lining of a seventeenth-century Welsh farmhouse built in Llangynydd.*
ABOVE, RIGHT: *The walls of the sixteenth-century Stryd Lydan barn in Wales.*

FAR RIGHT: *Plaited bamboo screen in a Vietnamese house.*
BELOW, LEFT: *Kirghiz nomads standing outside their* yurt *on the steppes of Central Asia.*
BELOW, RIGHT: *Bamboo bridge across the Siang River in the Indian state of Arunachal Pradesh.*

ASSEMBLING A *YURT*

be loaded onto two camels, but provides a home for a whole family. The walls are comprised of a collapsible lattice of larch or poplar to which the roof poles are tied. The walls are then lined with reed matting and covered with layers of felt.

Bridges

M ANY structures other than homes are built using basketry techniques. Some of the most impressive are suspension bridges which in northeast India, for example, are sometimes equipped with retaining walls and a walkway of interlaced bamboo.

TRANSPORT

Basketry is fundamentally light and is therefore an ideal component of anything that must be pulled, pushed or carried.

Sledges

The most primitive form of transport is the sledge which consists of a light framework on a pair of solid runners. In existence since prehistoric times, bamboo sledges, or *paragos*, with a basketry top are still in daily use in the north of the Philippines.

The nomadic tribes of the North American Plains were frequently on the move as they followed the herds of buffalo. Their goods were dragged behind their horses on a *travois*, a simple sledge made from rawhide and tent poles.

Litters

Litters, or palanquins, carried between men or horses must be as light as possible and so their frames have sometimes been made from basketry. Tent-like structures with a frame covered with textiles were once commonly erected on the backs of camels in Central Asia to transport women, especially at weddings.

Carts and chariots

Plaited or wicker sides and roofs for carts and chariots have been used for thousands of years. Stone reliefs from Assyrian times clearly depict wicker chariots and Julius Caesar himself wrote in *The Gallic Wars* about the efficacy of the light wicker chariots used by the Ancient Britons. Farm carts with wicker sides were still in use in parts of Hungary in the early twentieth century. In the burning heat of Chad the metal bodies of Citroën cars have sometimes been replaced with basketwork for added air conditioning.

LEFT: *Litters and palanquins made using basketry techniques have the advantage of being light. This toy* doolie, *complete with passenger, was made from sikki grass in Bihar, India.*
BELOW, LEFT: *Magyar herdsmen on the Hortobágy Plain in Hungary at the end of the nineteenth century. Nearby stands a farm cart with wicker sides.*
BELOW: *A hand-drawn delivery cart with basketry sides; discovered in an English antique shop.*

Prams and bathchairs

THE young, the old and the invalid may all need help moving around and in one form or another – the pram or bathchair – basketry has come to the rescue, although now the burden has mainly been taken over by tubular steel.

Baskets in the air

FOR thousands of years man has travelled through the air with the aid of enormous kites or in baskets hung from hot-air balloons. In the 1950s successful experiments took place in Manila to investigate the use of woven strips of bamboo for making cheap, light skins for aeroplanes!

ABOVE: *Children's toy prams. The larger is made of willow and the smaller of rattan.*
BELOW: *The lightweight basket used by balloonists is strong, but flexible enough to absorb the shock of a landing.*

TOP LEFT: *Processional cart with a plaited roof at Wat Doi Sutep temple in northern Thailand.*
LEFT, CENTRE: *New Yorkers relaxing at Long Beach promenade on Long Island during the 1920s.*
LEFT: *Toddler secure in an English copy of a Dutch bicycle seat.*

BOATS

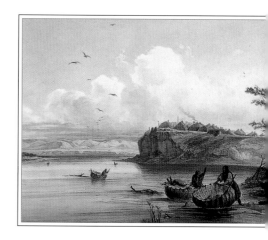

SOME of the greatest ocean voyages were made with the aid of basketry. The English adventurer Tim Severin, for one, proved that the legends about St Brendan crossing the Atlantic, in a leather-covered Irish *curragh*, more than a thousand years ago, in search of the Isles of the Blest, might well be true. While, on his 'Ra' expeditions in the 1960s, Thor Heyerdahl proved a reed boat was sufficiently seaworthy to cross the Atlantic from Morocco to the Caribbean.

AN EGYPTIAN REED BOAT, AFTER A PAINTING ON THE FIFTEENTH-CENTURY BC TOMB OF SENNUFER IN THEBES

Coracles

CORACLE is the Welsh word for a round, portable boat with a basketry frame-work covered in cowhide. Now more often covered in canvas, these one-man craft are ideal for fishing in fast-flowing rivers. Similar vessels called *paracils* are found in India and *curraghs* in Ireland, and in the USA George Catlin saw the Mandan Indians of North Dakota using such boats in the 1830s.

The Iraqi *quffa*, used on the Tigris, is a masterpiece which is constructed like a large, very tightly woven hex-weave basket

Reeds and rushes

GROWING on the edges of lakes and rivers, reeds and rushes make handy boatbuilding materials, although the life expectancy of the product is quite short as they eventually become waterlogged. Bundles of reed or rush can be fastened together to make a vessel shaped like a giant banana. Such vessels were used on the Nile by the Ancient Egyptians and on Clear Lake in California by the Pomo and can still be seen on Lake Chad in West Africa and Lake Titicaca in South America.

OPPOSITE, TOP RIGHT: *Mandan tribespeople sailing coracles on the Missouri; painted by Karl Bodmer on his travels between 1832 and 1834.*
OPPOSITE, ABOVE, LEFT: *The return of Manco Capec, the last Inca emperor, re-enacted at a festival on Lake Titicaca in South America.*
OPPOSITE, BELOW, LEFT: *Sailing* Scirpus totora *boats on the Desaguadero in southern Bolivia.*
OPPOSITE, BOTTOM RIGHT: *A coracle covered in tarpaulin; ones like this were used in the Ironbridge area on the River Severn in the west of England.*

covered in naturally occurring bitumen. In fact, the word 'quffa' actually translates as 'basket'. They may be large enough to hold twenty people.

Sails

MATTING is commonly used to make sails. It could once be seen on Chinese junks, the whaling boats of the Indonesian island of Lembata, and on Maori canoes. Two thousand years ago the Polynesians plaited fine sails from pandanus for the outriggers in which they made epic voyages, sailing thousands of miles across the Pacific Ocean.

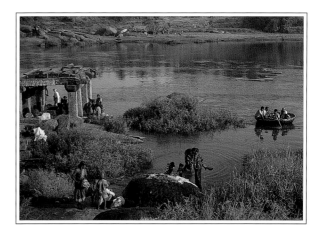

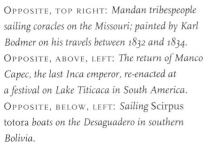

ABOVE, LEFT: *Cowhide-covered coracle with a frame of willow and hazel made by Kay Johnson in the style of those used on the River Teme in Herefordshire, England.*
TOP RIGHT: *A boy in the west of Ireland carrying a* curragh *with a split birch frame.*
LEFT: *Bitumen-covered* quffa *on the River Tigris.*
RIGHT: *Indian paracils at Hampi in Karnataka.*

Houseboats

THE rivers of Indochina are home to countless families living in floating houses. Many of these 'sampans' are equipped with a sliding roof made of a frame covered in bamboo matting.

FIVE

HATS

The problem of how to protect the head from the rain and sun has been solved in many ingenious ways by using the materials available. To this day, a handy palm frond may be employed as an impromptu umbrella or sunshade, but with a few deft twists the leaflets can be interlaced to form a crude disposable hat. Hats are produced all around the world, constructed using local materials and basketry techniques. Many now serve as status symbols or fashion accessories.

ABOVE: *Twined hat made from baobab bark and palm leaf, worn by the Senufo of the Ivory Coast.*
BELOW: *Plaited hat of brightly dyed sedge from Madagascar.*

Bamboo hats

IN all the countries where bamboo thrives, this versatile fibre is used to make hats that give protection against tropical downpours, as well as providing valuable shade.

Strips of bamboo are interlaced in a number of ways to create hats that are most typically conical, although some have a cylindrical or hemispherical crown. Frequently, they are made up of two layers with banana leaves or oiled paper sandwiched between them.

Straw hats

HATS of coiled, plaited straw have been common in Europe for centuries. Elaborate versions have been an enduring women's fashion accessory, worn on formal occasions such as weddings, but in their simpler forms, straw or grass hats have become increasingly popular as summerwear due to health scares concerning the sun's rays.

Palm hats

HATS of palm or pandanus are most often constructed by plaiting or coiling plaited strips in all the world's tropical and subtropical regions. Many different hats or 'sombreros' are made in Latin America. Now an export item, the 'panama' hat received its name from the location where it was first encountered by Europeans and North Americans during the building of the Panama Canal. It is actually made from pandanus fibre in Colombia and Ecuador where it is known as 'Jipijapa' after the town reputed to make the finest.

TOP: *Rattan Karen hat from northern Thailand. Banana leaves are sandwiched between two layers of hexagonally plaited rattan. The patina is created by smoke.*
ABOVE: *Itinerant Buddhist monks playing the shakuhachi (a bamboo flute) whilst begging were once a common sight in Japan, their faces concealed by a basket hat to maintain a distance from the material world.*

Twined hats

TWINED hats of grass or bark are woven in Saharan and subsaharan West Africa. Native Americans on the northwest coast of Canada and the USA make fine twined hats from grass and roots. These may be painted with clan totems or decorated with rings on the top which denote status.

LEFT: *Twined savannah grass hat from Ghana.*
BELOW: *Twined Fulani hat, from the Sahel of West Africa, decorated and reinforced with pieces of leather.*

BELOW: *Soulful Mexican musicians wearing sombreros of coiled palm-fibre plaits.*

FOOTWEAR

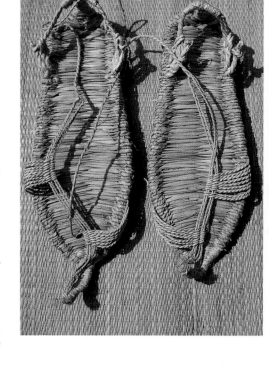

FOOTWEAR made of locally available plant fibres may not be the longest lasting, but it is cheap and easily replaced.

Soles

THE most basic use of basketry in shoemaking is in the manufacture of soles. Plaited and coiled plant fibres are still used to make light, everyday footwear such as Spanish espadrilles, or Colombian alpargatas. These are held on to the foot either by a broad strap across the front of the foot or by a pair of thongs coming up between the two largest toes, one passing to each side of the foot.

Sandals

FOR comfort and a better fit, straps, cords or thongs can be attached to the sole and wrapped over the foot and round the ankle. The Incas made sandals from aloe fibre, while the Japanese once preferred sandals of rice straw, called *zori*, when undertaking a long walk. As walking was the main mode of transport in feudal Japan, wayside shops generally had a stock of *zori* so travellers could replace worn out sandals.

The Japanese also make straw shoes for horses and cattle to protect their hoofs on stony roads.

Slippers

THE twining or plaiting of a toecap on to a sole creates a slipper, while continuing the process right around the sole will make a proper shoe. The twined grass slippers of Vietnam and the rush

TOP LEFT: *Nepalese twined hemp and grass shoe.*
CENTRE, LEFT: *Chinese twined rush shoe.*
ABOVE, RIGHT: *Chinese straw sandals.*

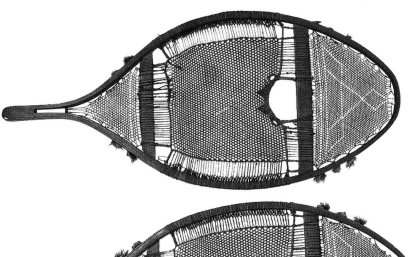

slippers of Thailand are obviously comfortable, but the plaited birch bark shoes made in Scandinavia are not so inviting, although they are much more flexible than wooden clogs.

Snow shoes

By spreading body weight over a large area, it becomes possible to walk more easily across snow. The Ojibway Indians who lived near the Great Lakes celebrated the first fall of snow each year with a special dance because once they were wearing their snow shoes, they could move faster than their prey and hunting was good.

The most familiar form of snow shoe is shaped rather like a tennis racquet strung with strips of rawhide. In Hungary, however, snow shoes were round and made of hazel.

OPPOSITE, BOTTOM LEFT: *Russian* lapti *made by plaiting the inner bark of the birch tree.*
OPPOSITE, BOTTOM RIGHT: *Twined grass slippers made in Vietnam.*
THIS PAGE, BOTTOM LEFT: *Twined rush slippers from Lamphun in northwest Thailand.*
BOTTOM RIGHT: *Twined rush sandals with plaited straps made in Lamphun, northwest Thailand.*
ABOVE, LEFT: *A pair of Danish plaited rush slippers.*
ABOVE, RIGHT: *Cree snowshoes, from Canada, strung with interlaced rawhide strips.*
RIGHT: *Eskimo hunter equipped with snowshoes.*

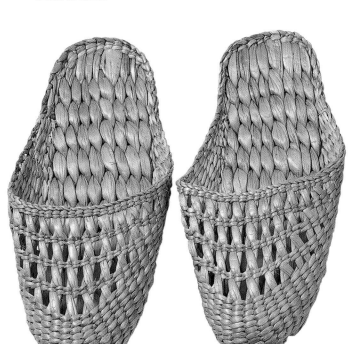

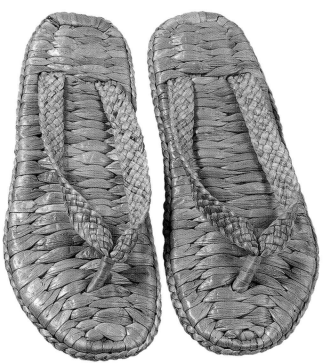

FIVE

FANS

POPULAR images of the use of fans include European ladies in crinolines and Japanese geisha girls in kimonos simpering behind collapsible fans of ivory, silk or paper, but in reality fans have been a vital tool in the everyday life of ordinary folk since before the Pharaohs ruled in Egypt.

Winnowing

ONE simple method of winnowing, which can still be witnessed in Sarawak, is to lift a basket of grain high up and pour it out onto a mat. As it falls, wafting gusts of air with a fan will blow away the chaff. The word 'fan' is actually derived from the Latin '*vannus*', a basket made especially for this purpose.

Fanning the flames

LIFE can be breathed into a fire with a fan which causes the flames to spread and the heat to rise. To concentrate the

FIVE

194

effect, fire fans are often small and tightly woven.

Cooling breezes

THE modern electric air-conditioning fan has its roots in the humble hand-held fan. Wafting cool breezes over oneself with a fan may seem decadent, but for many people in many parts of the world it is essential. The Hawaiian islanders have always used fans, but after their conversion to Christianity they found that long hours of sitting in a stifling church was made more tolerable by using fine pandanus fans. The stiffer and tighter the fan was woven, the stronger the draught it could make.

In India a large rectangular fan called a *punkah*, often made of matting, is hung from the ceiling. A servant or *punkah wallah* was often employed to sit and pull a rope that kept the fan in motion.

The language of fans

THE adoption of the fan as a fashion accessory in eighteenth-century Europe was accompanied by the development of a system of subtle gestures to communicate furtively with one's admirers. This was no new thing and fans have been used as part of the regalia of traditional dancers all over the world.

However, the language of fans has not only been romantic – the Japanese Samurai warlord, watching a battle from his stool, directed the ebb and flow of his bloody battalions with the movements of his fan.

OPPOSITE, TOP RIGHT: *Palm and leather fan from Maradi village, Niger.*
OPPOSITE, INSET: *Tongan woman with a fan.*
OPPOSITE, MAIN GROUP: *Four plaited fans bought in southern Thailand.*
THIS PAGE, MAIN GROUP: *clockwise from top left, twined grass, Ghana; plaited straw, China; coiled palm fibre, Sri Lanka; plaited palm, Lombok.*
ABOVE, RIGHT: *Large fire fan at a Blue Hmong hill-tribe village in northern Thailand.*
RIGHT: *Fan plaited from a single palm leaf, Ghana.*

WARFARE

Baskets have been used by soldiers on the move to carry their equipment since ancient times. Wickerwork back packs were used by both the Greek and Roman armies and during the Second World War millions of panniers were commissioned by the British War Ministry to hold essential supplies dropped from aeroplanes. But basketry has also been used in the actual cut and thrust of battle – for scabbards, the bindings of weapons and even armour.

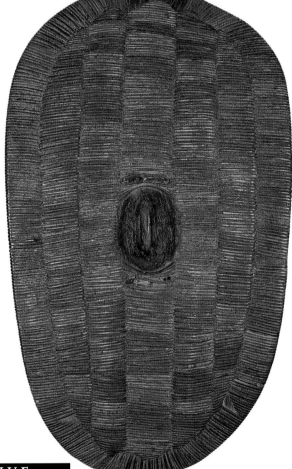

Defence

Dozens of coiled, twined and wicker shields from all around the world are on show at the Pitt Rivers Museum in Oxford, England. Roman legionaries practised with wicker shields, in Indochina they made bucklers of coiled rattan and in Tibet fighting men hung one round bamboo shield in front and one behind 'to confuse the enemy'.

Armour of cane, or wooden slats, held together with twined cords was used in the intertribal wars of the American West coast, while Pacific islanders once made body armour and helmets from woven coconut fibre and the pre-Incan Tiwanaku in the South Central Andes made helmets of cane stitched with camelid fibre.

Siege warfare

During the Middle Ages European and Japanese archers and sappers

Above: *Tutsi wicker shield with a wooden boss; made in Rwanda or Uganda in about 1900.*
Right: *A Mongo tribesman, armed with spear and coiled shield, escorting his wife through the jungle in Portuguese West Africa (now Angola).*

ASSYRIAN SIEGE ENGINE, AFTER A STONE RELIEF, FROM NIMRUD, DATING FROM 865–860 BC

CRUSADERS USING A *TREBUCHET*, FROM THE THIRTEENTH-CENTURY *HISTOIRE D'OUTREMER*

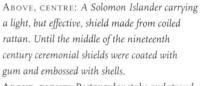

undermining the walls of fortresses were protected by wicker screens. Artillery required larger defences, and before the introduction of sandbags, the solution was *gabions*, huge wicker cylinders which were filled with earth.

Siege engines were used by the Assyrians nearly 3,000 years ago. They were equipped with archers and battering rams and covered in wicker panels. Thirteenth-century French manuscripts show crusaders using a *trebuchet*, a kind of large catapult. Missiles such as rocks or severed heads (intended to demoralize the enemy) were placed into a basket at the back and then hurled over the city walls.

Chariots

THE speed and mobility of chariots was a significant factor in the expansion of many ancient empires. Light chariots with wicker sides were developed by the Egyptians to fight the Hyksos, while chariots were later used to great effect by the Etruscans and the Celts, who managed to repulse Julius Caesar from Britain.

Basket cases

IN the First World War bodies too badly damaged to be carried off on a stretcher were removed in a basket which is where the expression 'basket case', meaning a hopeless cause, is derived from.

ABOVE, CENTRE: *A Solomon Islander carrying a light, but effective, shield made from coiled rattan. Until the middle of the nineteenth century ceremonial shields were coated with gum and embossed with shells.*

ABOVE, RIGHT: *Rectangular stake and strand shield from Cameroon.*

BELOW, LEFT: *War and peace on the Gilbert Islands in the Pacific. The waistcloth (left) was constructed from pandanus fibre and the body armour (right) was made from tightly worked coconut fibre.*

BELOW, RIGHT: *German minerwerfer being loaded on the Western Front during the First World War. On the right are the baskets used for transporting shells.*

OPPOSITE, TOP RIGHT: *Split-cane bindings on a throwing spear from the Indonesian island of Sumba.*

OPPOSITE, MIDDLE RIGHT: *A bolo, heavy multi-purpose knife used in the Philippines, with a split-cane grip around the metal handle.*

OPPOSITE, BOTTOM RIGHT: *An early twentieth-century shield carried by the Mongo, a Bantu-speaking tribe from Portuguese West Africa (now Angola).*

TOYS

PLAY is preparation for adulthood. Children learn to use their senses and develop manipulative skills. Through play they explore the mysterious world of adults.

Rattles

ONE of the first toys to delight babies is the rattle, a hollow form containing a few beans or seeds, which makes an exciting noise whenever the infant shakes it. This is perhaps the first item over which a small child has total control (until it is thrown out of the pram). Brightly coloured or invitingly shaped, rattles are made everywhere, frequently using the skills of a basketmaker.

Dolls and animals

EARLY companions, such as dolls and toy animals, share a child's joy and pain and are often the victims of cathartic outbursts. Many of these replicas merely consist of deftly twisted straw, but are alive in the imagination.

FIVE

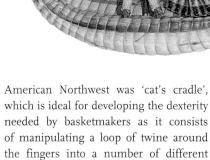

American Northwest was 'cat's cradle', which is ideal for developing the dexterity needed by basketmakers as it consists of manipulating a loop of twine around the fingers into a number of different configurations.

In Mexico great fun is derived from *tragadedos* (finger swallowers) and *pescanovias* (sweetheart traps). These are simple plaited tubes of brightly dyed palm strips with a cord at one end which is pulled to tighten the trap around the finger of an unsuspecting friend. In Bogotá, Colombia, they are called *robamuchachas* and are used as part of courtship.

Miniatures

Traditionally, children's toys include imitations of the paraphernalia of their parents such as weaving equipment or shopping bags for girls and fishing and hunting gear for boys. They are scaled down, so that children can learn the skills they will one day need by emulating their parents.

Tiny versions of familiar objects are also the tools of imaginative play and these, too, objects like boats, flocks of animals and furniture, are designed to reflect daily life.

Games

Interactive games may also involve the manipulation of fibres and fabrics. One of the most popular games played in the

Opposite, above, left: *Coiled grass dolls from Bihar, India.*

Opposite, top right: *Child's shopping basket of straw plaits; made in China.*

Opposite, right centre: *Toy cradle, from the Philippines, made from coco ribs.*

Opposite, bottom right: *Plaited pandanus rattle from Tamil Nadu, India, and Zulu grass rattle from South Africa.*

Above, left: *Kenyan twined grass doll rattle.*

Above, centre: *Split-palm leaf rattle from Mali.*

Top right: *Toy* totora *boat, from Peru, with a crew of grass dolls from Ecuador.*

Right: *Mexican 'finger traps' made from brightly dyed palm strips.*

Inset, right: *Kiwai child, from Papua New Guinea, playing 'cat's cradle', a popular pastime everywhere from Australia to Alaska.*

LEISURE

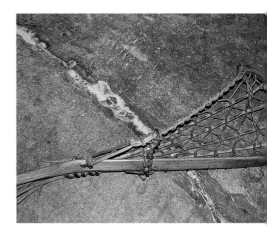

T HE use of baskets has reduced the time and effort required for daily work. This time is often spent enjoying pastimes in which basketry objects play a central part.

Sport

I N the Ancient world contests of strength, fitness and guile were used to hone hunting and fighting skills. Many modern games require a racquet, but many old games such as the ball games played by the Choctaw and other tribes of the American Southeast required sticks with a woven scoop on the end. This was the origin of lacrosse, a game often associated with schools for young ladies today.

In 1891 Dr James Naismith was asked to invent a non-contact game for students at the YMCA Training School in Springfield, Massachusetts. He nailed a peach basket 3 metres (10 ft) above the ground at each end of a court and invented basketball.

An informal, but popular, game is played worldwide by a small group who try to keep a ball in the air as long as possible without using their hands. In Southeast Asia the ball is traditionally made of interlaced rattan.

In Britain during the eighteenth century singlestick became a popular form of exercise. It was a type of fencing in which the two combatants fought with a stick fitted with a basketwork hand guard.

ABOVE: *A wooden lacrosse stick with a rawhide basket.*

Gambling

Games of chance are popular with many Native Americans, and a particularly popular diversion among the Californian tribes involved throwing dice into a large flat tray made specifically for the purpose. The dice were made from walnut shells or acorns split in half and points were scored according to the number of flat surfaces uppermost.

Music

Baskets can even be used as musical instruments. Many rattles are made with basketry and upturned coiled baskets were once used as drums by the Navajo.

Opposite, centre: *A willow basket used for transporting the stone used in curling, a Scottish winter sport played on a frozen loch or river.*
Opposite, bottom: *Interlaced rattan balls made in Thailand, where they are used to play takraw. The game is popular all over Southeast Asia, including Indonesia, where it is known as sepek raga.*
Above, left: *A Native American coiled gambling tray, on which dice were thrown, from California.*
Above, right: *Snake charmers on a street in Tamil Nadu, southern India.*

Holidays

Many Westerners love to spend their holidays lying on a beach in an exotic location. Expensive hotels often provide their visitors with shade cast by rustic umbrellas and all around the world beach-side shops carry a stock of cheap, reed beach mats.

Below, left: *Twined grass decorations made in Montecristi, an important hat and basketmaking centre in Ecuador.*
Below, right: *Mexican decorative dyed palm balls.*

FIVE

BASKETRY AS ART

Traditional societies, such as the Inuit of northern Canada, often had no word corresponding to 'art'. Everything they made had a practical use and yet care was lavished on carving and decorating the most mundane objects such as boots, combs or hats. The decoration may have served a magical purpose, suggested status or revealed vanity, but the idea of an object serving a purely aesthetic function was anathema.

Style

In Japan, after centuries of political upheaval and feuding, the peaceful climate of the Edo period in the seventeenth century meant that the powerful could use their wealth to sponsor artists and craftsmen. The purism of the Zen philosophy, which invented the Tea Ceremony, and scrupulous attention to detail were applied to many functional items to give them a beautiful and deceptively simple style that has been described as 'artful artlessness'. They became 'works of art'. The principles were applied to basketry, often allowing the form to emphasize the nature of the materials as can frequently be seen in many *ikebana* (flower arranging) baskets.

The 'new basketry'

During the twentieth century plastic, wire and industrial production methods have created substitutes for traditional basketry. When the restrictions of functionalism were lifted some basketmakers and other artists began to investigate the use of basketmaking techniques in the creation of sculpture and art objects. During the 1970s this became a movement, spearheaded by Ed Rossbach,

Above: *Japanese nineteenth-century bamboo ikebana* basket. Kohōsai, the maker, was declared a 'living national treasure'.
Below, left: *A basket of plaited wattle bark made by Mika McCann, a Japanese basketmaker living in the USA.*
Below, right: *A stake and strand basket of different-coloured willow barks; made by Molly Rathbone.*

Professor of Design at the University of California in Berkeley and author of several influential books. The barriers between basketry and art were broken down as exciting new forms and concepts were explored. Artists became basketmakers and basketmakers became artists and the relationship between art and craft was challenged.

ABOVE, LEFT: *Basket of birch bark strips made by Mary Butcher.*
BELOW: *'Willow Ripple', a site-specific sculpture by Mary Butcher for Blickling Hall in Norfolk, England.*

Recycled materials

Rossbach himself made baskets from newspaper, plastic and polythene – the use of recycled materials has become a particularly dynamic aspect of the movement. But this approach does not merely display a fascination with the vibrancy of contemporary waste products, it is also a conscious statement about the fragility of the environment and the damage we cause. In spirit, Lois Walpole, whose materials are discarded plastic and card from the streets of London, is not as far away as it might appear from generations of basketmakers, such as the Aleutian basketmakers mentioned in the introduction, gathering materials from the world outside their back doors.

FIVE

TOP: *Rattan motorbike from Ubud in Bali.*
ABOVE, LEFT: *'Stacking laundry baskets' made by Lois Walpole from willow, painted card and dyed cane.*
ABOVE, RIGHT: *'Fisherman', a living willow sculpture by Claire Guest.*

COLLECTING BASKETS

ABOVE: *Hats and baskets for sale at Kali market, Guizhou, China.*
LEFT: *A market in Peru; in the foreground are twined baskets from Huacho.*
BELOW, LEFT: *Hardware shop, in Petchaburi, Thailand, stocked with baskets for every function.*

WHAT TO BUY

WHEN buying a basket there are several factors to be taken into consideration, but first and foremost you should buy one that you find appealing. If you are buying baskets abroad, there are arguments both for and against buying those made specifically for the tourist trade. If you buy well-made traditional items rather than those made cheaply to sell to tourists then you will help keep traditional basketmaking alive, but equally many baskets made to be sold to tourists are well crafted and are the only source of income available to their makers. When buying old baskets it is important to examine them carefully. It is probably worth repairing structural damage to domestic and everyday baskets, but antiques and museum quality items should be left as they are, although you can always get professional advice. It is seldom worth acquiring them if they have woodworm as you may be putting the rest of your collection at risk.

WHERE TO BUY

Whenever possible you should buy a basket directly from the maker. This way you can learn more about the basket and probably pay less for it and all of the money you pay will go directly to the maker. When buying baskets abroad, you should look further than the tourist shops and markets if you can – look for hardware stores or basketmakers' workshops where the locals buy their baskets. In the West, some high street shops operate a Fair Trade policy and may sponsor basket production by cooperatives around the world. These baskets are often standardized, but the quality is generally quite reasonable. Importers specializing in

craftwork can be found in many towns offering one-off items. A wide range of international basketry, particularly from Africa and the USA, can also now be found on the internet. But it is well worth hunting for bargains in bric-à-brac and charity shops as the value of baskets is often not recognized.

LOOKING AFTER YOUR BASKETS

Too much heat will make baskets brittle and strong sunlight will cause colours to fade. Most baskets need no more attention than occasional dusting, but natural-coloured baskets intended for daily use and made of materials such as willow will benefit from a rinse in warm water on a fine day and being left to dry in the shade. Excellent advice on repairs and conservation can be found in *The Complete Book of Baskets and Basketry* by Dorothy Wright.

ABOVE, LEFT: *Barotse (Lozi) coiled baskets from the collection of Barry Trice.*
ABOVE, RIGHT: *Zulu baskets for sale at Sky Fire in Jerome, Arizona, USA.*
BELOW, LEFT: *Tutsi baskets collected by London-based textile dealer Clive Loveless.*
BELOW, RIGHT: *Fine basketry and other crafts at the Night Market in Chiang Mai, Thailand.*

Glossary

alpagartas Colombian sandals, similar to espadrilles, with braided hemp or pita fibre soles and cotton uppers and straps.

ambong Duffel bag made in Sarawak from plaited rattan.

'arm' basket Rigid basket carried in the hand or on the arm by a stout handle; often used for shopping.

'ato Polynesian basket made by plaiting the leaflets of an intact palm frond. The *'ato* is then cut open to release the contents.

awl A pointed metal spike, or bodkin, used to make openings in the fabric of a basket.

axis (plural: axes) The direction in which fibres are worked, e.g., horizontally, vertically, diagonally, or obliquely.

babiche Long thin strips cut from rawhide.

bango (pronounced 'bongo') Back pack made by the Ifugao of the northern Philippines.

basket weave Plain weaving, over one, under one.

bast Fibres, such as hemp or linen, obtained from the stems of certain herbaceous plants.

bilum All-purpose bag of looped fibres, from New Guinea.

bolo Heavy knife used in the fields in the Philippines.

border Reinforced rim of a basket.

broken rice Malay name for tightly woven triaxial plaiting.

brown willow Dried willow rods with their bark intact (not necessarily brown in colour).

buff willow Willow rods that have been dyed by boiling before their bark is stripped off.

bunchung A lunch box used by the Monpa of Arunachal Pradesh, northeast India, consisting of a pair of tightly fitting plaited hemispheres.

burden basket Heavy duty back pack.

butt Thick end of a rod from the end nearest to the base of the plant.

buttocks basket Frame basket with two distinct bulges.

cabalitto (Spanish for 'little horse') A Peruvian boat of bundled reeds.

calabash A large gourd, often used to hold water.

cane 1. The long, tough stems of bamboo and certain woody reeds such as *Arundo donax*; 2. Rattan.

carrizo Spanish for *Arundo donax*, a bamboo-like reed.

cattail The American name for reed mace, *Typha latifolia*, the false bulrush.

centre cane Material from the centre of a rattan stem; also called pith cane, pulp cane or, in the USA, reed.

century plant Agave.

charpoy Indian bed strung with rawhide or twine.

checkerwork Plain plaiting, over one, under one.

chip A small basket or punnet made from plaited veneer.

chocalatillo Small fibrous plant growing in the Amazon and Orinoco basins of South America.

cleave 1. Verb: to split lengthways; 2. Noun: a device with three or four fins used to split willow into skeins.

coppicing Pruning trees and shrubs heavily to encourage the growth of long pliant stems suitable for basketmaking.

coracle Round, portable Welsh boat with a basketwork frame covered in hide; see also curragh.

courge A frame basket used by Guernsey fishermen to hold live bait.

cow-wiss (curlicue or porcupine twist) Textured decoration used by the Algonquian tribes of the American Northeast; created by twisting elements on the surface of a basket.

cran Basket used to hold herrings. It has a capacity of approximately 180 kg; the quarter cran was once the most widely used fish basket in the British Isles.

creel Fisherman's basket usually worn on the hip.

cundu A flexible openweave, plaited basket made by the Waunana people of the Colombian Chocó.

curragh The Irish equivalent of the coracle (see above), built in a more recognizable boat shape.

cyntell Welsh frame basket woven from willow and used to harvest potatoes.

dao A multi-purpose knife carried by tribal peoples in northeast India.

dextral In oblique plaiting, an element running from bottom left to top right. In Iban baskets dextrals are often dyed.

dilly bag A soft, multi-purpose gathering bag used by Australian Aborigines.

English randing Interweaving one weaver at a time in and out of vertical stakes round the basket.

fitching The twining method used in stake and strand basketry; also called reverse pairing. A Z twist is produced.

foundation The warp material of a coiled basket, which is stitched into a spiral.

frail or flail A basket made from a coil of plaited rushes; used by British agricultural workers to carry their lunch.

French randing Randing with a number of weavers, one starting at each stake.

gabion Large wicker cylinder filled with earth or rocks to prevent landslip, or as a defensive shield for artillery.

God's eye, or 'ojo de dios' An elaborate lashing at the join of the two hoops of a frame basket.

green willow Freshly cut willow which is green because it is heavy with sap.

grig An unbaited eel trap used in the Fens of eastern England.

güerregue *Werregué* palm.

harakeke Maori word for New Zealand flax, *Phormium tenax*.

hen basket (or ose) Ancient type of frame basket made of concentric hoops drawn together at the top to make a handle. Thought to have been invented in Scotland. Known in Germany as a 'rocking boat'.

hex weave/hexagonal weave Plaiting on three axes which creates a pattern of hexagons or triangles.

hive 1. Man-made nest for bees; 2. Baited eel trap used in the English Fens.

hobuk A sheath made by the Adi Gallong of Arunachal Pradesh, northeast India.

igiseke Small coiled grass baskets made by the Tutsi in Rwanda, Uganda and Tanzania.

imbenge Originally a Zulu coiled basket inverted to cover a clay beer pot, but may also now refer to telephone-wire bowls made in South Africa.

iraca Term used in Central America for *Carlodovica palmata*, pandanus.

isichumo Zulu coiled basket used to carry water.

isithebe Zulu rush mat employed in the preparation and serving of food.

jewel basket Feather-covered basket made by the Pomo of California.

karui Japanese hexagonal weave back pack.

kete Maori bag made from plaited *harakeke* (see above).

kiddle A large English fish trap, now illegal. This is where the English saying 'a fine kettle of fish' is derived from.

kiondo Round 'shopping' basket made in Kenya from twined sisal.

kishie Carrying basket from the Shetland Islands, usually used to carry peat; made from oat straw or dock stalks.

Klikitat People living on the Columbia River, Washington State, in the USA. Often used as a blanket term to describe the imbricated baskets of other tribes from the Northwest coast.

kong khao Container for carrying cooked rice; from Thailand.

kophi An elaborate burden basket woven by the Angami Naga of Nagaland, northeast India.

koppit Man's expanding, lidded basket used by the Bontoc and Ifugao of the northern Philippines.

lapti Russian shoes of plaited inner birch bark.

lauhala Hawaiian word for pandanus leaves.

lipwork Basketry made from coiled straw. The technique was once used to make 'seed lips' for broadcasting seed.

Lloyd Loom Basketmaking company who produced a variety of furniture made from twisted paper.

mad weave Tightly woven hexagonal plaiting.

Madeira side An English term for trac weave (see below).

maguey Sisal, the fibres extracted from agave.

'melon' basket A frame basket with a handle.

messob Table used as part of wedding rites in the Shoa district of Ethiopia.

mochila Maguey bags (see above) worn in pairs by Arhuaco men in north Colombia.

Monaco border French term for trac weave (see below).

mudah Northeast Indian stool made from bamboo and cane.

mura A stool similar to the *mudah* (above), made from *jhunda* grass in Haryana State, northern India.

oblique plaiting Plaiting on a diagonal or bias.

ojo de dios ('God's eye') Magical symbol of the Huichol of northwestern Mexico which gives its name to elaborate lashings on frame baskets.

olla Large jar-shaped basket used by the White Mountain Apache to store grain.

ose See hen basket.

osiers Long pliable willow shoots suitable for basketmaking.

overlay Material laid on the surface of one set of structural elements to produce a decorative effect.

pairing Stake and strand technique, the opposite of fitching (see above); produces an S twist.

panier à jour French 'everyday' shopping basket.

pannier Pair of bags or baskets, often slung over animals.

paracil Indian version of the coracle (see above).

pescanovia ('sweetheart trap') Mexican fingertrap made from an elastic tube of plaited palm.

picking off Removing protruding ends from a finished basket.

pith cane or pulp cane Weaving material from the centre of rattan; called reed in the USA.

pitting Keeping cut willow rods alive by standing them in water.

pottle A small fruit basket.

pricking up Pricking a rod with an awl (see above), so that it can be bent without breaking. A technique used in upsetting stake and strand baskets.

prickle A wicker fruit basket, once made from briars.

quffa Iraqi coracle-style boat.

quirt Short whip used by horsemen.

randing The basic weaving technique used in stake and strand basketry, over one, under one.

rapping iron A heavy tool for beating tight the weave of a stake and strand basket.

reed 1. A plant growing in damp places, of the genera *Phragmites* or *Arundo*; 2. the American term for rattan centre cane.

rib Structural element added to the hoops of a frame basket before weaving.

ribbed basket A frame basket; the name refers to the conspicuous ribs.

rive To split a log into splints.

robamuchacha ('girl catcher') Colombian word for a finger trap.

rocking boat In German *Schiffsswingen*, a hen basket.

rod Long pliant material used in basketmaking.

S twist Fibres plied or twisted together in an anti-clockwise direction.

saung Balinese knife sheath made from a borassus palm leaflet.

scallom A long tapering cut which forms a tongue on the butt of a rod.

sciathóg Irish frame basket for straining potatoes.

screw-pine English term for pandanus – the leaves grow up the stem in a spiral.

seagrass Sedge leaves plied into cord, used mainly for chair seating.

selok A basket worn at the hip, in Sarawak, while sowing rice.

sepak raga Indonesian game in which a group of players keep a rattan ball in the air for as long as possible without using their hands.

shigra Looped agave fibre bag made in Ecuador.

shook Scottish frame basket used to hold baited fishing lines; also called a scull or scoo.

sika Coiled basket, from Bangladesh, made from a single coiled rod of rattan.

sinistral An element running from bottom right to top left, in oblique plaiting.

sintong Basket used in Sarawak when harvesting rice.

sisal Coarse fibres extracted from agave, a large succulent indigenous to arid regions in the Americas.

six-way caning Plaiting on three axes which produces a pattern of hexagons; used in chair seating.

skeins Fine strips made by cleaving and shaving peeled willow rods.

skep A bee hive made from coiled straw.

slath The start of a stake and strand basket consisting of a cross formed from two sets of rods at right angles to each other.

slewing Randing using two or more weavers in tandem, sometimes called double weave.

slype Flat or slanting cut.

spale, spelk, spell or splint Wood split into flat strips for basketmaking.

spill A fine, flat strip of wood or cane.

stake Structural rod that forms part of a basket's skeleton. The passive warp element of a stake and strand basket.

strand (or weaver) The active weft woven between the stakes of a stake and strand basket.

swill Large basket; in different parts of Britain the name is applied to baskets with a variety of structures and functions.

takraw Thai word for the *sepak raga* game (see above).

takul A plaited Balinese basket for carrying a fighting cock.

tendle A frame basket for collecting oysters; made in East Mersea, Essex, England, from green elm saplings.

tiffin basket Box or basket used to carry a light meal.

topinambour French basket of nailed wooden slats for collecting Jerusalem artichokes.

trac weave Basket wall or border with an open weave in which all the elements are active as they interlace with each other going up, are bent over and then interlace on the way back down.

tragadedo 'Finger swallower', a Mexican finger trap.

triaxial Worked on three axes; also called hex weave.

tsero Ilala palm winnowing basket from Zimbabwe; may be twined or stake and strand.

tump-line A strap that fits across the forehead; used to carry burden baskets.

tutup Food cover of brightly dyed pandanus made in the southern Philippines.

upsetting The act of driving stakes into the base, in stake and strand basketry, and bending them up to form the walls of a basket.

wale A strong band, in stake and strand basketry, worked with three or more weavers passed, in a staggered sequence, over several strands and under one.

warp The passive element in basketmaking, i.e., in coiled basketry, the foundation material; in stake and strand basketry, the stakes.

wattle 1. A panel of interlaced willow or hazel; 2. Common name in Australia for plants of the genus *Acacia*.

wattle and daub Wall created by smearing mud or dung on an interlaced hazel panel.

weave 1. Verb: to interlace fibres when making a basket; 2. Noun: the interlaced structure of a basket.

weaver (or strand) Pliant rod interlaced in and out of the more rigid stakes.

weft The active element in basketmaking, i.e., in coiled basketry, the stitches; in stake and strand basketry, the strands; in plaited basketry, both sets of elements.

werregué Leaflets of the *werregué* palm are used by the Waunana of the Colombian Chocó in the manufacture of finely stitched coil baskets.

white willow Willow rods peeled after harvesting or after pitting.

wicker Materials such as willow used in wickerwork.

wickerwork Stake and strand basketry.

withy A flexible willow rod; sometimes used specifically for the osier willow *Salix viminalis*.

Z twist Fibres plied or twisted together in a clockwise direction.

zori Japanese straw sandal fastened with a straw thong.

ACKNOWLEDGMENTS

This book would not have been possible but for the work of the many basketmakers, some well known but many anonymous, whose work is featured.

First of all I must express my gratitude to Polly Gillow who devoted considerable time and effort to this book, making many valuable contributions, and who has had to cope with my obsessive personality all this time.

Particular thanks are owed to Mary Butcher for her generosity in providing expert knowledge, advice and encouragement and for the loan of baskets and photographs. Clive Loveless opened some very useful doors and shared his enthusiasm for African basketry, while I have been able to feature many interesting baskets because of access to the collections of Barry Trice, Peter Collingwood, Kay Johnson and my friend John Gillow (aka the Brigadier).

Many people allowed me to view their collections, permitted photography or provided photographs, while many others shared valuable information. I would like to thank Denny Abbey, Nicholas Alberry, Robyn Badley, Allen and Renee Barraza, The Basketmakers Association, Ian Beaty, Rosie Bose, Ruth Bowers, Tarin Brokenshire, Todd Calhoun, Cameron Trading Post, Amanda Cashmore, Suleyman Cetin, Peter and Elizabeth Collingwood, Ilay Cooper, David De'Ath, Malcolm Dodson, David Edmonds, David Goff Eveleigh, John Fredericks, Lisa Geller, Rachel Geller, Luke Gillow, Peter Gillow, Alan Gray, Gwydir Street Antiques (Cambridge), Janet Harvey, Jonas Hasselrot, Jonathan Hope, Hubbell Trading Post, Alastair and Hazel Hull, Katie Jones, Owen Jones, Phil King, Julie Last, Trevor Leat, The High Commission of the Kingdom of Lesotho, Colin Manthorpe, Andy McKay, Sheila Paine, Chris Patel, Yvonne Pedretti, Pioneer Village Trading Post, John Richardson, Riverside Antiques (Ely), Carl Sadler, Alan and Joan Sentance, Paul and Christine Sentance, Judy Simpson, Sky Fire in Jerome, Sergei Stanyukovich, Roddy Taylor, Karun Thakar, Ullapool Museum, Lois Walpole, Ian West, Jocelin Whitfield, Dennis Woodman, and Ped Young.

Museums and Collections

AUSTRALIA
Adelaide
South Australian Museum
North Terrace
Adelaide
South Australia (5000)
Tel. (08) 82077500
Aboriginal, Oceanic and South-East Asian collections

BELGIUM
Dilsen-Stokkem
Maaspark Negenoord
Rechtestraat 7
3650 Dilsen-Stokkem
Tel. (01) 1755016
Open-air museum with basket displays

Tervuren
Musée de l'Afrique Centrale
Royal
13 Steenweg op Leuven
3080 Tervuren, Brabant
Tel. (02) 7695211
Central African baskets

BRAZIL
Rio de Janeiro
Museu do Indio
Rua das Palmeiras 55
Botafogo
Rio de Janeiro 22270-070
Tel. (021) 2862097
Brazilian Native American collection

CANADA
Vancouver
Museum of Anthropology
c/o University of British
Columbia
6393 Marine Drive NW
Vancouver, British Columbia
V6T 1Z2
Tel. (604) 822 5087

CHINA
Beijing
Museum of the Cultural
Palace of National Minorities
Changan Street
100 000 Beijing
Hill-tribe collection

Guiyang
Guizhou Provincial Museum
Beijing Road
Guiyang
550 000 Guizhou
Miao, Dong and Shwe collection

COLOMBIA
Bogotá
Museo Etnografico de
Colombia
Calle 34
No. 6–61 piso 30
Apdo. Aéreo 10511
Bogotá
Colombian folk collection

THE DEMOCRATIC REPUBLIC OF CONGO (FORMERLY ZAIRE)
Kinshasa
Museum of Ethnology and
Archaeology
Université National du Congo
B.P. 127, Kinshasa

CZECH REPUBLIC
Prague
Náprstkoro Muzeum
asijskych, africkych a
americkych kultur
(Náprstkoro Museum
of Asian, African and
American Culture)
Betlemské nám 1
11000 Prague
Tel. (02) 22221416

DENMARK
Copenhagen
Nationalmuseet (National
Museum)
Prinsens Palais
Frederiksholms Kanal 12
1220 Copenhagen
Tel. 33134411
*Ethnographic collections.
Fine seventeenth-century
African baskets*

FRANCE
Cadenet
Musée de la Vannerie
La Glaneuse
Avenue Philippe de Girard
84160 Cadenet
Tel. 04 90 68 24 44
Basketry museum

Paris
Fondation et Musée Dapper
50 avenue Victor Hugo
75016 Paris
Tel. 01 45 00 01 50

Musée de l'Homme
Palais de Chaillot
17 place du Trocadéro
75116 Paris
Tel. 01 44 05 72 72
*Worldwide ethnographic
collection, including baskets
from Mali and Ethiopia*

Musée National des Arts
d'Afrique et d'Océanie
293 avenue Daumesnil
75012 Paris
Tel. 01 44 74 84 80
African and Oceanic collection

Vallabrègues
Musée de la Vannerie
5 rue Carnot
30300 Vallabrègues
Tel. 04 66 59 23 41
Basketry museum

GERMANY
Berlin
Museum für Völkerkunde
Staatliche Museen zu Berlin –
Preußischer Kulturbesitz
Lansstrasse 8
14195 Berlin
Tel. (030) 2660
*Worldwide ethnographic
collection*

Beverungen
Korbmacher-museum
Dalhouse der Stadt
Beverungen
Lange Reihe 23
37688 Beverungen
Tel. 05645 1823
Comprehensive displays

Michelau
Deutsches Korbmuseum
Bismark Strasse 4
96247 Michelau
Tel. 09571 83548
Extensive basket display

Munich
Staatliches Museum für
Völkerkunde München
Maximilianstr 42
80538 Munich
Tel. 089 21 01360
*Ethnographic collection,
including Tutsi baskets*

Stuttgart
Linden-Museum Stuttgart-
Staatliche Museum für
Völkerkunde
Hegelplatz 1
70174 Stuttgart
Tel. (0711) 2022408
*Central Asian and Oceanic
collection*

HUNGARY
Budapest
Néprajzi Múzeum
(Ethnographic Museum)
Kossuth Lajos tér 12
1055 Budapest
Tel. (01) 3326340
*Hungarian ethnographic
collection*

Kecskemét
Szórakaténusz Játékmúzeum
(Szórakaténusz Toy Museum)
Gáspar András ú 11
6000 Kecskemét
Tel. (076) 481469
*Large basketry collection,
including rushwork*

JAPAN
Osaka
Kokuritsu Minzokugaku
Hakubutsukan (National
Museum of Ethnology)
10–1 Senri Banpaku Koen
Suita-Shi
Osaka 565–8511
Tel. 06 876 2151

MALAYSIA
Kuching
Sarawak Museum
Jalan Tun Haji Openg
93566 Kuching
Sarawak
Tel. (082) 44232
Iban crafts

MEXICO
Mexico City
Museo Nacional de Artes e
Industrias Populares del INI
Avenida Juárez 44
06050 Mexico City
Tel. (05) 5103404
*Important collection of Native
American traditional crafts*

NETHERLANDS
Leiden
Rijksmuseum voor
Volkenkunde (National
Museum of Ethnology)
Steenstraat 1
2312 BS Leiden
Tel. (071) 5168800
*Indonesian and South-East
Asian collections*

Rotterdam
Museum voor Volkenkunde
(Museum of Geography and
Ethnology)
Willemskade 25
3016 DM Rotterdam
Tel. (010) 2707172
*Indonesian and South-East
Asian collections*

NEW ZEALAND
Auckland
Auckland Institute and
Museum
Auckland Domain
Auckland 1000
Tel. (09) 3090443
*New Zealand and Oceanic
collection*

Wellington
Te Papa, Museum of New
Zealand Te Papa Tongarewa
Cable St
Wellington 6020
Tel. (04) 3817000
*New Zealand, Hawaii and
Oceanic collection*

PAPUA NEW GUINEA
Port Moresby
National Museum and Art
Gallery
Waigini
Port Moresby

PERU
Lima
Museo Nacional de
Antropologia y Arqueologia
Plaza Bolivia s/n
Pueblo Libre
Lima
Tel. (01) 635070

PHILIPPINES
Manila
National Museum of
the Philippines
P. Burgos St
Rizal Park
1000 Manila
Tel. (02) 5271215
*Philippine folk and tribal
collection*

POLAND
Warsaw
Muzeum Azji i Pacyfiku (Asia
and Pacific Museum)
ul. Solec 24
00-467 Warsaw
Tel. (022) 6296724

PORTUGAL
Lisbon
Museu Etnográfico da
Sociedade de Geografia de
Lisboa (Ethnographical
Museum)
Rua Portas de Santo Antão
100
1150-269 Lisbon
Tel. 213425401
*Asian, African and South
American collections*

RUSSIA
St Petersburg
Muzej Antropologii i
Etnografii im. Petra Velikogo
(Peter the Great Museum
of Anthropology and
Ethnography)
Universitetskaja Nab 3
199034 St Petersburg
Tel. (812) 3280712
Asian collection

SOUTH AFRICA
Cape Town
South African Cultural
History Museum
49 Adderley St
PO Box 645
Cape Town
Tel. (021) 4618280
*African, Asian and European
collection*

SPAIN
Barcelona
Museu Etnològic
(Ethnography Museum)
Parque de Montjuic
08038 Barcelona
Tel. 934246402
*Worldwide ethnographic
collection*

Madrid
Museo Nacional de Etnologia
(Ethnography Museum)
Alfonso XII, 68
28014 Madrid
Tel. 915306418
*Worldwide ethnographic
collection*

SWEDEN
Gothenburg
Etnografiska Museet
(Ethnography Museum)
Norra Hamngatan 12
41114 Gothenburg
*African, South American,
Lapp and South-East Asian
collections*

Kalmar
Kalmar Läns
Skälby gård
392 38 Kalmar
Tel. (048) 012111
Ethnographic collection

Karlstad
Värmlands Museum
Sandgrund
651 08 Karlstad
Tel. (054) 143100

Luleå
Norrbottensmuseum
Storg 2
951 08 Luleå
Tel. (0920) 243500
Sami ethnography

Stockholm
Folkens Museum
Etnografiska (National
Museum of Ethnography)
Djurgårdsbrunnsvägen 34
102 52 Stockholm
Tel. (08) 51955000
*Worldwide ethnographic
collection*

Friluftmuseet Skansen
(Skansen Open Air Museum)
Djurgården
115 93 Stockholm
Tel. (08) 4428000
*Open-air museum with
reconstructed buildings*

Nordiska Museet
(The National Museum
of Cultural History)
Djurgårdsv. 6–16
115 93 Stockholm
Tel. (08) 51956000

Umeå
Västerbottens Museum med
Svenska Skidmuseet
Gammlia
906 03 Umeå
Tel. (090) 171800

SWITZERLAND
Brienz
Schweizerisches
Freilichtmuseum Ballenberg
(Ballenberg Rural Museum)
3855 Brienz
Tel. 033 9521030
*Baskets and working basket-
maker*

Wohlen
Freiämter Strohmuseum
Kirchenplatz
5610 Wohlen
Tel. 056 62260626
*Straw plaits, ornaments
and hats*

THAILAND
Bangkok
Kamthieng House
The Siam Society
131 Soi Asoke
Sukhumvit Road 21
Bangkok 10110
Tel. (02) 66164707
*Traditional Thai farming and
fishing implements and baskets*

Chiang Mai
Hill-tribe Museum and
Research
Rama 9 Park
Chotana Road
Chiang Mai
Tel. 210872, 221933
Thai hill-tribe crafts

UNITED KINGDOM
Anstruther
Scottish Fisheries Museum
Saint Ayles
Anstruther KY10 3AB
Tel. 01333 310628
*Baskets related to the fishing
industry*

Bath
The American Museum
in Britain
Claverton Manor
Bath BA2 7BD
Tel. 01225 460503
*Chairs and baskets, mostly
Native American*

Cambridge
Cambridge and County Folk
Museum
2–3 Castle Hill
Cambridge CB3 0AQ
Tel. 01223 355159
Local baskets and eel traps

Cardiff
Museum of Welsh Life
St Fagans
Cardiff CF5 6XB
Tel. 02920 573500
*Includes reconstructions and
re-creations of buildings dating
from Celtic times onwards*

Castel, Guernsey
Guernsey Folk Museum
Saumarez Park
Castel
Guernsey
Channel Isles GY1 7UJ
Tel. 01481 55384
*Traditional domestic and
agricultural basketry*

Dereham
Norfolk Rural Life Museum
Beech House
Gressenhall
Dereham
Norfolk NR20 4DR
Tel. 01362 860563
*Reconstruction of basketmaker's
workshop, tools and baskets*

Farnham
Rural Life Centre
Reeds Road
Tilford
Farnham GU10 2DL
Tel. 01252 792300
Willow, cane and rush work

Glastonbury
Somerset Rural Life Museum
Abbey Farm
Chilkwell Street
Glastonbury BA6 8DB
Tel. 01458 831197
Traditional rural baskets

Gloucester
Gloucester Folk Museum
99–103 Westgate Street
Gloucester GL1 2PG
Tel. 01452 526467
River fishing baskets

Great Yarmouth
Great Yarmouth Museums
Galleries
Tolhouse Street
Great Yarmouth NR30 2SH
Tel. 01493 745526
*Basket work related to the
fishing industry*

Halifax
Bankfield Museum
Akroyd Park
Boothtown Road
Halifax HX3 6HG
Tel. 01422 354823
*Worldwide and contemporary
basketry*

Kew
Department of Economic
Botany
Kew Palace and Museums of
the Royal Botanic Gardens
Kew TW9 3AB
Tel. 020 8940 1171
*Collection of ethnographic items
illustrating plant use*

Lincoln
Museum of Lincolnshire Life
Old Barracks
Burton Road
Lincoln LN1 3LY
Tel. 01522 528448
*Mainly willow basketry, with
some cane, rush and straw work*

London
The British Museum
Great Russell Street
London WC1B 3DG
Tel. 020 7636 1555
*Worldwide ethnographic
collection formerly housed
at the Museum of Mankind
in London*

Horniman Museum
100 London Road
Forest Hill
London SE23 3PQ
Tel. 020 8699 1872
*Worldwide ethnographic
collection*

Luton
Luton Museum
Wardown Park
Luton LU2 7HA
Tel. 01582 746722
*Good collection of straw plait
work*

Stockwood Craft Museum
and Gardens
Stockwood Park
Farley Hill
Luton LU1 4BH
Tel. 01582 38714
Willow and rush baskets

Oxford
Pitt Rivers Museum
South Parks Road
Oxford OX1 3PP
Tel. 01865 270927
*Extensive ethnographic
collection (take a torch!)*

SOURCES OF ILLUSTRATIONS

Reading
Museum of English Rural
Life
Whiteknights
Reading RG6 2AG
Tel. 0118 931 8660
*The largest collection of English
country baskets. Ring before-
hand if you wish to view the
extensive reserve stock*

Stowmarket
Museum of East Anglian Life
Abbot's Hall
Stowmarket IP14 1DL
Tel. 01449 612229
*Complete basketmaker's
workshop and traditional
basket collection*

UNITED STATES OF AMERICA
Augusta, Maine
Maine State Museum
Library-Museum-Archives
Bldg
State House Complex
Augusta, ME 04333-0083
Tel. (207) 287 2301

Cambridge, Mass.
Peabody Museum of
Archaeology and Ethnology
11 Divinity Av
Cambridge, MA 02138
Tel. (617) 496 1027

Cherokee, North Carolina
Cherokee Indian Reservation
Cherokee
North Carolina

Chicago, Illinois
Field Museum of Natural
History
Roosevelt Road at Lake Shore
Drive
Chicago, IL 60605
Tel. (312) 922 9410

Denver, Colorado
Denver Art Museum
100 W 14th Av Pkwy
Denver, CO 80204
Tel. (303) 640 4433

Dragoon, Arizona
The Amerind Foundation
2100 N Amerind Road
Dragoon, AZ 85609
Tel. (520) 586 3666

Eureka, California
The Clarke Memorial
Museum
240 E Eureka St
Eureka, CA 95501
Tel. (707) 443 1947

Flagstaff, Arizona
Museum of Northern Arizona
3101 N Fort Valley Road
Flagstaff, AZ 86001
Tel. (520) 774 5213

Goldendale, Washington
Maryhill Museum of Art
35 Maryhill Museum Drive
Goldendale, WA 98620
Tel. (509) 773 3733

Haines, Alaska
Sheldon Museum
11 Main St
Haines, AK 99827
Tel. (907) 766 2366

Honolulu, Hawaii
Bishop Museum
1525 Bernice Street
Honolulu, HI 96817-0916
Tel. (808) 847 3511

Klamath Falls, Oregon
Favell Museum of Western
Art and Indian Artifacts
125 West Main St
Klamath Falls, OR 97601
Tel. (541) 882 9996

Los Angeles, California
Southwest Museum
234 Museum Drive
Los Angeles, CA 90065
Tel. (213) 221 2163

New York
American Museum of Natural
History
Central Park West at 79th
Street
New York, NY 10024
Tel. (212) 769 5100

National Museum of the
American Indian
Smithsonian Institution
George Gustav Heye Center
1 Bowling Green
New York, NY 10004
Tel. (212) 514 3700

Norris, Tennessee
Museum of Appalachia
Hwy 61
Norris, TN 37828
Tel. (423) 494 7680

Phoenix, Arizona
The Heard Museum
2301 North Central Avenue
Phoenix, AZ 85004
Tel. (602) 252 8840

Santa Fe, New Mexico
Wheelwright Museum of
the American Indian
704 Camino Lejo
Santa Fe, NM 87505
Tel. (505) 982 4636

Second Mesa, Arizona
Hopi Cultural Centre
Second Mesa
Hopi Reservation, AZ 86043
Tel. (520) 734 6650

Sitka, Alaska
Sheldon Jackson Museum
104 College Drive
Sitka, AK 99835
Tel. (907) 747 8981

Spokane, Washington
Cheney Cowles Museum
2316 First Avenue
Spokane, WA 99204
Tel. (509) 456 3931

Tucson, Arizona
Arizona State Museum
University of Arizona
Tucson, AZ 85721-0026
Tel. (520) 621 6281

Ukiah, California
Grace Hudson Museum
and the Sun House
431 S Main Street
Ukiah, CA 95482
Tel. (707) 467 2836

Window Rock, Arizona
Navajo Nation Museum
Window Rock
Navajo Reservation, AZ 86515
Tel. (520) 871 6673

Yosemite, California
Indian Cultural Museum
Museum Bldg
Yosemite National Park
Yosemite, CA 95389
Tel. (209) 372 0281

The following abbreviations have been used: *a*, above; *b*, below; *c*, centre; *l*, left; *r*, right; *t*, top

Unless otherwise stated all drawings are by Bryan Sentance

James Austin 1, 3, 5, 7*l*, 8, 17*a*, 20*ar*, 21*al*, 22*b*, 23*ar*, 25*ar*, 25*br*, 26*bl*, 29*b*, 29*c*, 32*b*, 35*b*, 37*t*, 38*tr*, 38*b*, 40*tl*, 41*tl*, 41*tr*, 41*cr*, 41*b*, 42*cr*, 43*t*, 45 all, 49*ar*, 49*b*, 51*al*, 52*b*, 53*r*, 55*ar*, 60*c*, 64*b*, 65*t*, 65*bl*, 66*b*, 67*t*, 68*b*, 69*a*, 69*bl*, 70*ar*, 72*bl*, 73*cl*, 73*br*, 75*t*, 78*c*, 80*bl*, 81*tl*, 82*bl*, 83*bc*, 83*br*, 84*cr*, 85*br*, 87*tl*, 87*br*, 88*b*, 91*a*, 93*ac*, 93*ar*, 96*al*, 96*br*, 97*r*, 98*cl*, 98*cr*, 99*b*, 100*br*, 102, 103*ar*, 103*br*, 104*ar*, 104*bl*, 104*br*, 105*ar*, 105*br*, 106*cl*, 106*cr*, 107*br*, 109*a*, 110*bl*, 110*br*, 111*tr*, 111*br*, 112*cr*, 113*ar*, 114*bl*, 115*tr*, 115*bl*, 118*cl*, 118*cr*, 121*c*, 121*b*, 125*a*, 127*l*, 129*al*, 129*bc*, 129*br*, 132*tr*, 132*br*, 133*al*, 134*b*, 137*bl*, 137*br*, 139*b*, 141*b*, 143*b*, 145*t*, 146*bl*, 146*br*, 147*b*, 155*l*, 156*ar*, 156*br*, 158*ar*, 158*bl*, 158*br*, 162*bl*, 163*tl*, 164*r* 2nd down, 164*bl*, 165*bl*, 165*br*, 167*c*, 169*r*, 170*l*, 171*tr*, 171*bc*, 173*tr*, 176*bl*, 181*c*, 187*ar*, 190*ar*, 190*al*, 191*r*, 192*bl*, 192*br*, 193*bl*, 193*br*, 194*c*, 194*b*, 195*t*, 195*c*, 196*al*, 198*br*; James Austin (from the Mary Butcher Collection) 21*b*, 24*br*, 25*br*, 27*a*, 28*a*, 28*b*, 29*t*, 30*l*, 31, 36*l*, 39*b*, 40*br*, 46*b*, 55*al*, 71*a*, 72*tr*, 76*l*, 77*t*, 78*b*, 83*a*, 99*a*, 106*b*, 114*br*, 115*br*, 130*bl*, 138*l*, 138*r*, 147*tl*, 147*cl*, 159*ar*, 165*a*, 166 all, 170*ar*, 171*al*, 177*ar*, 190*bl*, 193*al*, 194*tr*, 199*al*, 199*ac*, 202*br*; Rosie Bose 204*ar*; Peter Collingwood 18*bl*, 78*l*, 140*t*, 142*ar*, 192*tl*, 192*cl*; Ilay Cooper 58*ar*, 145*bl*, 184*tr*, 185*br*, 189*br*; Kim Fielding 172*b*; Lee Funnell with the permission of Mary Butcher 82*br*, 144*b*, 175*ac*; John Gillow 18*tl*, 19*al*, 58*bl*, 63*cr*, 70*br*, 87*bl*, 88*br*, 94*cl*, 95*al*, 95*tr*, 123*cr*, 141*al*, 183*ar*, 184*cr*, 184*bl*; Polly Gillow 19*bl*, 47*tc*, 81*bl*, 134*al*, 135*al*, 145*cr*, 156*cl*, 160*ar*, 163*bl*, 171*cr*, 180, 186*br*, 188*br*, 204*bl*, 205*br*; John Hammond with the permission of Jonathan Hope 111*l*; Jonas Hasselrot 103*cl*, 178*bl*, 178*bc*; Richard Heeps 2, 20*bl*, 65*cr*, 92, 96*bl*, 160*br*, 191*al*; with permission of the High Commission of Lesotho 157*b*; with the permission of the Imperial War Museum, London 197*br*; Mark Irving 187*bl*; Kay Johnson 11*b*, 19*tr*, 68*ar*, 126*ar*, 162*cr*, 174*br*, 175*tr*, 182*c*, 188*al*, 204*al*; Phil King 175*br*; Trevor Leat 179*b*; with the permission of Clive Loveless 196*l*; Bryan Sentance 6*bl*, 7*ar*, 7*br*, 10 all, 11*al*, 11*ar*, 14 all, 15*l*, 15*br*, 17*bl*, 17*br*, 18*lc*, 18*ac*, 18*ar*, 19*rc*, 19*br*, 21*ar*, 21*br*, 22*ar*, 23*tl*, 23*cl*, 23*br*, 24*tr*, 24*cl*, 24*bl*, 26*ar*, 27*b*, 30*ar*, 30*r*, 32*a*, 33 all, 34 all, 35*l*, 35*a*, 35*cr*, 36*ar*, 36*br*, 37*cr*, 37*br*, 38*c*, 39*al*, 40*bl*, 41*cl*, 42*b*, 43*c*, 43*cb*, 43*br*, 44*l*, 44*br*, 46*ar*, 47*tl*, 47*tr*, 47*cr*, 47*b*, 48 all, 49*al*, 50 all, 51*ar*, 51*b*, 52*a*, 53*al*, 53*bl*, 54 all, 56, 57 all, 58*al*, 59*ar*, 59*bc*, 60*ar*, 61*al*, 61*cr*, 62*b*, 63*t*, 63*c*, 63*bl*, 63*bc*, 64*ar*, 66*ar*, 69*br*, 70*ac*, 70*bl*, 71*cl*, 71*cr*, 72*cr*, 72*br*, 73*tl*, 73*tc*, 73*tr*, 73*bl*, 74*bl*, 74*br*, 75*b*, 76*ar*, 77*c*, 77*cr*, 77*br*, 79 all, 80*ar*, 80*cr*, 81*c*, 81*br*, 84*t*, 84*bc*, 85*tc*, 85*tr*, 85*c*, 85*bl*, 86*r*, 86*bl*, 87*tr*, 87*c*, 88*ar*, 89 all, 90 all, 91*br*, 93*bc*, 93*br*, 94*tl*, 94*ar*, 94*br*, 95*b*, 96*ar*, 97*l*, 98*tl*, 98*tr*, 98*bl*, 100*tl*, 100*tc*, 100*tr*, 100*bl*, 101 all, 103*tl*, 104*l*, 105*al*, 106*tr*, 107*al*, 107*tr*, 107*bl*, 108 all, 109*bl*, 110*al*, 110*ar*, 112*tr*, 113*bl*, 113*br*, 114*ar*, 115*al*, 116 all, 117 all, 118*tr*, 119*tl*, 119*tc*, 119*tr*, 119*b*, 120, 121*tl*, 121*tc*, 121*tr*, 122*al*, 122*ar*, 122*bl*, 123*al*, 123*br*, 124*cr*, 124*b*, 125*bl*, 125*br*, 126*bc*, 127*cl*, 127*br*, 129*tc*, 129*cr*, 130*tr*, 131 all, 133*cr*, 133*br*, 134*cr*, 135*tr*, 135*cr*, 135*br*, 136 all, 137*tl*, 137*ar*, 139*t*, 139*cl*, 140*cr*, 140*bl*, 140*br*, 141*ar*, 142*al*, 142*bl*, 143*al*, 144*tr*, 144*c*, 145*cl*, 145*br*, 146*tr*, 146*c*, 147*tr*, 148 all, 149 all, 150*tr*, 150*cl*, 150*bl*, 151 all, 153*tr*, 153*bl*, 153*bc*, 153*br*, 154 all, 155*tr*, 155*cr*, 155*br*, 156*tl*, 156*bl*, 157*l*, 157*ar*, 158*c*, 159*al*, 159*cl*, 159*br*, 160*l*, 161*tl*, 161*tr*, 161*cl*, 161*cr*, 161*br*, 163*cr*, 163*br*, 164*al*, 164*tr*, 164*r* 3rd down, 164*b*, 167*al*, 167*tr*, 167*b*, 168*c*, 168*cr*, 168*l*, 168*br*, 169*bl*, 170*br*, 171*br*, 172*tr*, 172*cl*, 172*cr*, 173*tl*, 173*tc*, 173*c*, 173*br*, 173*bl*, 174*ar*, 174*bl*, 176*c*, 176*br*, 177*b*, 179*tl*, 181*tl*, 181*tr*, 181*cr*, 182*ar*, 183*cl*, 183*br*, 186*cl*, 187*tl*, 189*al*, 192*ar*, 193*tr*, 195*tr*, 195*br*, 196*cr*, 196*br*, 197*tr*, 198*l*, 198*tr*, 198*cr*, 199*tr*, 199*rc*, 200 all, 201*al*, 201*bl*, 201*br*, 202*ar*, 202*bl*, 203*tr*, 203*cr*, 203*bl*, 205*al*, 205*ar*, 205*bl*; with the permission of the Smithsonian Institution, Washington, D.C. 12*br*, 31*br*; Mike Squire 185*al*, 185*tr*; Karun Thakur 162*t*; Tumi 16; Lois Walpole 55*b*, 203*cl*; Mike Waterman (from the Mary Butcher Collection) 6*ar*, 24*br*, 25*l*, 25*br*, 37*c*, 61*br*, 84*bl*, 128*br*, 177*al*, 177*c*, 203*al*; Jocelin Whitfield 187*br*; reproduced from *Aboriginal Indian Basketry* by O. T. Mason 9*ar*, 12*l*, 12*b*, 15*ar*, 119*cl*, 179*tr*; reproduced from *Indian Basketry* by G. W. James 13*br*, 124*tl*, 124*cl*, 144*tl*.

Bibliography

Materials

Farrelly, David, *The Book of Bamboo*, Thames & Hudson, London, 1996

Lambeth, M., *A Golden Dolly, The Art, Mystery and History of Corn Dollies*, John Baker, London, 1969

Lee, Molly, *Baleen Basketry of the North Alaskan Eskimo*, North Slope Borough Planning Department, Barrow, Alaska, 1983

Paul, Frances, *Spruce Root Basketry of the Alaska Tlingit*, Sheldon Jackson Museum, Sitka, Alaska, 1944

Ranjan, M. P., Nilam Iyer, Ghanshyam Pandya, *Bamboo and Cane Crafts of Northeast India*, National Institute of Design, New Delhi, 1986

Staniforth, Arthur, *Straw and Straw Craftsmen*, 2nd edn, Shire, Princes Risborough, 1981

Techniques

Barratt, Olivia Elton, *Basket Making*, Letts, London, 1990, and Henry Holt, New York, 1993

Bird, Adren J., Steven Goldsberry, J. Puninani Kanekoa Bird, *The Craft of Hawaiian Lauhala Weaving*, University of Hawaii Press, Honolulu, 1982

Butcher, Mary, *Willow Work*, Dryad Press, London, 1986

Collingwood, Peter, *The Maker's Hand: A Close Look at Textile Structures*, Interweave Press, Loveland, Co., 1987, and Bellew Publishing Company, London, 1998

Crampton, Charles, *Cane Work*, Dryad Press, Leicester, 1948

Fitch, Barbara, *Decorative Straw Craft*, Search Press, Wellwood, UK, date unknown

Gabriel, Sue, and Sally Goymer, *The Complete Book of Basketry*, David and Charles, London, 1991

Griswold, Lester, *Handicraft, Simplified Procedure and Projects*, 9th edn, Prentice-Hall, New York, 1952

Harvey, Virginia I., *The Techniques of Basketry*, University of Washington Press, London and Seattle, 1986

Heseltine, Alastair, *Baskets and Basketmaking*, Shire, Princes Risborough, 1982, 1996

Johnson, Kay, *Basketmaking*, Batsford, London, 1991

Lambeth, M., *Discovering Corn Dollies*, Shire, Princes Risborough, 1987, 1994

Ng, Mary, *Natido Binwag Weaves the Bango*, Council For Living Traditions, Manila, 1978

Roffey, Mabel, *Simple Basketry*, Pitman, London and New York, 1930

Sekijama, Hisako, *Basketry: Projects from Baskets to Grass Slippers*, Kodansha International, New York and Tokyo, 1986

Seymour, John, *The Forgotten Arts, A Practical Guide to Traditional Skills*, Dorling Kindersley, London, 1984

Traditional Crafts in Britain, Reader's Digest Association, London, 1982

Verdet-Fierz, Bernard and Regula, *Willow Basketry*, Interweave Press, Loveland, Co., 1993

Walpole, Lois, *Creative Basket Making*, Collins, London, and North Light Books, Cincinnati, Ohio, 1989

———, *Weave Coil and Plait Crafty Containers from Recycled Materials*, Search Press, Wellwood, UK, 1997

Wright, Dorothy, *The Complete Book of Baskets and Basketry*, David and Charles, Newton Abbot, 1977

Places of origin

Arbeit, Wendy, *Baskets in Polynesia*, University of Hawaii Press, Honolulu, 1990

Bléhaut, Jean-François, *Iban Baskets*, Sarawak Literary Society, 1994

Brandford, Joanne Segal, *From the Tree Where the Bark Grows: North American Basket Treasures from the Peabody Museum*, Harvard University, Cambridge, Mass., 1984

Braun, Barbara (ed.), text by Peter G. Roe, *Arts of the Amazon*, Thames & Hudson, London and New York, 1995

Campbell, Margaret, Nakorn Pongnoi, Chusak Voraphitak, *From the Hands of the Hills (Thai hilltribe crafts)*, Media Transasia, Hong Kong, 1978, 1981

Clarke, Duncan, *African Hats and Jewellery*, Grange Books, Rochester, 1998

Coe, Ralph T., *Sacred Circles: Two Thousand Years of North American Indian Art* (Catalogue of exhibition at the Hayward Gallery, London), Arts Council of Great Britain, 1976

Cooper, Ilay, and Barry Dawson, *Traditional Buildings of India*, Thames & Hudson, London and New York, 1998

Cooper, Ilay, and John Gillow, *Arts and Crafts of India*, Thames & Hudson, London and New York, 1996

Cort, Louise, and Nakamura Kenji, *A Basketmaker in Rural Japan*, Smithsonian Institution, Washington, D.C., in association with Weatherhill, New York and Tokyo, 1994

Davies, Lucy, and Mo Fini, *Arts and Crafts of South America*, Thames & Hudson, London, 1994, and Chronicle Books, San Francisco, 1995

Dawson, Barry, and John Gillow, *The Traditional Architecture of Indonesia*, Thames & Hudson, London and New York, 1994

DeWald, Terry, *The Papago Indians and their Basketry*, DeWald, Tucson, Arizona, 1979

Eisman, Jr, Fred B., *Ulat-Ulatan, Traditional Basketry in Bali*, White Lotus, Bangkok, 1999

Feest, Christian F., *Native Arts of North America*, Thames & Hudson, London and New York, 1992

Grossert, J. W., *Zulu Crafts*, Shuter & Shooter, Pietermaritzburg, 1978

Hasselrot, Jonas, *Korgar, Tradition Och Teknik*, Lts förlag, Stockholm, 1997

Hiroa, Te Rangi (Peter H. Buck), *Arts and Crafts of Hawaii*, section iv, Twined baskets, Bishop Museum Press, Honolulu, 1964

Hrdlička, Zdeněk, and Venceslava Hrdlicková, *The Art of Japanese Gardening*, Hamlyn, London, 1981

James, George Wharton, *Indian Basketry*, Dover Publications, New York, 1901, 1909, 1972

Jones, Suzi (ed.), *Pacific Basket Makers, A Living Tradition* (catalogue), University of Alaska Museum, Fairbanks, Alaska, 1981

Lane, Robert E., *Philippine Basketry, An Appreciation*, Bookmark Inc., Manila, Philippines, 1986

Lobb, Allan, *Indian Baskets of the Northwest Coast*, Charles H. Belding, Portland, Oregon, 1978, 1990

Mason, Otis T., *Aboriginal Indian Basketry*, Rio Grande Press Inc., Glorieta, New Mexico, 1902, 1972

Menten, Theodore, *Japanese Border Designs*, Dover Publications, New York, 1975

Mowat, Linda, Howard Morphy and Penny Dransart (eds), *Basketmakers: Meaning and Form in Native American Baskets*, Pitt Rivers Museum, Oxford, 1992

Munan, Heidi, *Sarawak Crafts*, Oxford University Press, Oxford and New York, 1989

Puketapu-Hetet, Erenora, *Maori Weaving*, Longman, Auckland, 1999

Sayer, Chloë, *Arts and Crafts of Mexico*, Thames & Hudson, London, and Chronicle Books, San Francisco, 1990

Sichel, Marion, *Japan* (National Costume Reference Series), Batsford, London, and Chelsea House, New York, 1987

Sieber, Roy, *African Furniture and Household Objects*, Indiana University Press, Bloomington and London, 1980

Starzecka, D. C. (ed.), *Maori Art and Culture*, British Museum Press, London, 1996, 1998

Dato'Haji Sulaiman Othman, et al., *The Crafts of Malaysia*, Archipelago Press, Singapore, 1994, 1997

Taylor, Colin F. (ed.), *The Native Americans*, Tiger Books International, Twickenham, 1995

Teiwes, Helga, *Hopi Basket Weaving, Artistry in Natural Fibres*, University of Arizona Press, Tucson, Arizona, 1996

Trowell, Margaret, *African Design*, Frederick A. Prager, New York, 3rd edn, 1971

Turnbaugh, Sarah Peabody, and William A. Turnbaugh, *Indian Baskets*, Schiffer Pub., West Chester, Pennsylvania, 1986

Villegas, Liliana, and Benjamin Villegas, *Artefactos: Colombian Crafts from the Andes to the Amazon*, Rizzoli, New York, 1992

Warren, William, and Luca Invernizzi Tettoni, *Arts and Crafts of Thailand*, Thames & Hudson, London, 1994, and Chronicle Books, San Francisco, 1996

Watson, William (ed.), *The Great Japan Exhibition: Art of the Edo Period, 1600–1868* (exhibition catalogue), Royal Academy of Arts, London, 1981

Wendrich, Willeke, *Basketry in Egypt: Ancient Traditions, Modern Applications* (Slide set), Manchester Metropolitan University, 1994

————, *The World According to Basketry: An Ethno-Archeological Interpretation of Basketry Production in Egypt*, C.N.W.S. Research School, Leiden, 1999

Whiteford, Andrew Hunter, *North American Indian Arts*, Golden Press, New York, 1973

————, *Southwestern Indian Baskets: Their History and Their Makers*, School of American Research Press, Seattle, 1988

History

Bahn, Paul G. (ed.), *The Atlas of World Archaeology*, Time-Life Books and Checkmark Books, New York, 2000

Bobart, H. H., *Basketwork through the Ages*, The Basketmakers' Association, 1997, 1st published in 1936 by Oxford University Press, London

Caselli, Giovanni, *The First Civilizations*, Macdonald, London, and P. Bedrick Books, New York, 1983

Ross, Anne, *Everyday Life of the Pagan Celts*, Batsford, London, and G. P. Putnam's Sons, New York, 1970

Segrelles, Vincent, *Weapons of the Past*, Frederick Warne, London, 1980

Shaw, Ian, and Paul Nicholson, *British Museum Dictionary of Ancient Egypt*, British Museum Press, London, 1995

Wilcox, Charlotte, *Mummies and their Mysteries*, Young Library, Corsham, and Carolrhoda Books, Minneapolis, 1993

General and miscellaneous

Basho, Matsuo (trans. Lucien Stryk), *On Love and Barley: Haiku of Basho*, Penguin, Harmondsworth, 1988, and University of Hawaii Press, Honolulu, 1985

Butcher, Mary, *Contemporary International Basketmaking* (exhibition catalogue), Merrell Holberton, London, 1999

Coote, Jeremy, Chris Morton and Julia Nicholson, *Transformations: The Art of Recycling* (Exhibition Catalogue), Pitt Rivers Museum, Oxford, 2000

Easton, M. G., *The Bible Dictionary*, Bracken Books, London, 1989

Gillow, John, and Bryan Sentance, *World Textiles: A Visual Guide to Traditional Techniques*, Thames & Hudson, London, and Bulfinch Press, Little Brown and Co., Boston, 1999

Herald, Jacqueline, *World Crafts: A Celebration of Designs and Skills*, Letts, London, 1992, and Lark Books, Asheville, North Carolina, 1993

Onions, C. T. (ed.), *The Oxford Dictionary of English Etymology*, Clarendon Press, Oxford, 1976, 1982

Rossbach, Ed, *Baskets as Textile Art*, Van Nostrand Reinhold, London and New York, 1973

————, *The New Basketry*, Van Nostrand Reinhold, London and New York, 1976

Schiffer, Nancy, *Baskets*, Schiffer Publishing Limited, Pennsylvania, 1984

Wilcox, R. Turner, *Folk and Festival Costume of the World*, Scribner, New York, 1965, and Batsford, London, 1989

INDEX